CELEBRITY SLAYINGS THAT SHOCKED THE WORLD

John Sanders

TRUE CRIME Library

NON-FICTION

True Crime Library
A Forum Press Book
by the Paperback Division of
Forum Design,
PO Box 158, London SE20 7QA

An Imprint of True Crime Library
© 2001 Mike James
All rights reserved

Typeset and cover design by Ben James
Printed and bound in Great Britain by
Cox & Wyman, Reading, Berkshire

ISBN 1 874358 39 7

PREFACE

We live in a world obsessed with wealth and celebrity, the twin icons of our age. Film and TV screens put the faces in front of us, newspapers and magazines tell us breathlessly how much they earn.

Celebrities used to be the great, the good and the wise. Not any longer. Today many of our idols have feet of clay. Anyone with a talent that sells, which is not necessarily great talent, can achieve a piece of fame. But because we all love looking at celebrities and reading about them, when one of them dies in mysterious circumstances we feel we have lost a friend.

Hollywood film-makers have probably done more to create the murder mystery than any other medium. But many of its own mysteries, although staged off the screen, have been within its own domain. For Hollywood, with its beautiful women, matinee idols, power-crazed moguls and dreamers, has the perfect set of ingredients for murder, mystery and scandal.

Some of the stories from the film capital would have made enthralling movies, but they were too close to home. And they happened to be true.

Some of them are among the stories in his book. They still intrigue, still puzzle. In every death there is a mystery until the cause is known. In Hollywood, with its propensity to close ranks during an investigation, too many causes remain a mystery.

In politics, murder is more often called assassination, but it is still murder. Every world leader is vulnerable to the assassin - even, as we report here, a British Prime Minister.

Film stars, singers, politicians, sportsmen, these are today's celebrities. When they die suddenly, violently, the world is stunned. They may have glittering lives - but there is sometimes a darker side...

TRUE CRIME LIBRARY

CONTENTS

1

MARILYN MONROE
Hollywood's Biggest-ever Cover-up

Marilyn Monroe was no more. The summer Sunday morning news of the death of Tinseltown's screen goddess at the age of 36 reverberated around the world with the impact of a major disaster.

The news flashes, carefully orchestrated by her studio's publicity department, revealed that she had committed suicide. Well, they added as a sort of afterthought, she had probably committed suicide.

Probably?

There were empty pill boxes beside her bed – one had contained Nembutal, a brand of sleeping pill, another had held chloral hydrate pills. Curiously, although the blonde bombshell, a pill addict, could never take her medicine without liquid, there was no sign of a glass anywhere in the bedroom.

Her naked body was face down on top of the bedclothes. This too was curious, because she always went to bed in a bra and night-dress. And when someone overdoses their body usually returns in reflex to the foetal position.

She never locked the bedroom door, although when the alarm was raised it was found to be locked. A doctor went round to the window (the bedroom was on the ground floor), broke the glass and got into the room. But the glass was also found on the ground outside the window, not on the carpet, which meant that it must have been broken from the inside.

Marilyn's live-in housekeeper Mrs. Eunice Murray said she began to think something was wrong when she saw the bedroom light was on – her mistress went to bed that night at 8 p.m. Mrs. Murray knew the light was on because there was a chink of light under the door.

But, everyone later agreed, the pile of Marilyn's bedroom carpet was so thick it would have been impossible to see a chink of anything under the door.

Marilyn probably died hours earlier on Saturday, August 5th, 1962, although the police were not called until 4.30 on Sunday morning. Her doctor, Hyman Engelberg, and psychiatrist, Dr. Ralph Greenson, had both got there before them. When they arrived somewhere between midnight and 3.30 a.m., the washing machine was whirring away in the kitchen. No one seemed to think that 3.30 a.m. is a funny time to be doing the washing, even in Hollywood.

The time of death on the death certificate was given as 3.50, at least eight hours after she died. Yet at 10.30 p.m. on Saturday night, that is, six hours before the police arrived, Arthur Jacobs, who was a publicist with Marilyn's studio, was at a Hollywood Bowl concert when he was asked to take a call from someone unknown. The caller said there was an emergency involving Marilyn Monroe and asked him to go at once to her home.

And at the post-mortem, carried out by a junior doctor, no trace of drugs was revealed in her stomach.

Suicide?

Of course it was suicide, the studio publicist, the police, the investigators, even the coroner, all chorused. Look at the facts. The career of the legendary Marilyn Monroe, born Norma Jean Baker, had been on the skids for some time, and everyone knew her personal life was in ruins too. The previous 18 months in particular were a chapter of disasters.

On January 20th, 1961, she was divorced amid some acrimony by her husband, Arthur Miller, the distinguished playwright. She had recently had an abortion – one of several, it was discovered at the post-mortem. On that occasion the potential father was unknown.

She was visiting her psychiatrist Dr. Greenson, and he was visiting her, on an almost daily basis, and was virtually dependent on drugs and barbiturates. Her emotional problems had reached such a pitch that she had been sacked from her latest film *Something's Got To Give* for absenteeism.

Physically and mentally exhausted she had been admitted – much against her will – to a psychiatric clinic in New York. Then she was rescued by her second husband Joe DiMaggio, the baseball star known as the "Yankee Clipper," who had her committed into his care.

As Norman Mailer would later write in her biography, "Marilyn was on a slide into the longest depression of her life."

So when the coroner of Los Angeles County, Dr. Theodore Curphey, issued a press release suggesting suicide the world at large was quite prepared to accept that, to forget the manner of her death and remember only the legend.

The press release was worded: "On the basis of information obtained, it is our opinion that the case is 'probably suicide' ... beside her bed was an empty bottle that had contained 50 Nembutal tablets. The presumption is that Marilyn took 47 of them at one time."

In fact, later investigators were to show, much of this was poppycock. On her last day alive, a Saturday, Marilyn Monroe was noted by friends to be cheerful. In the afternoon she sat by the pool reading film scripts under offer to her. With her was her best friend, Pat Newcomb, who had stayed overnight at Marilyn's house on Friday night and spent most of that Saturday with her.

While it was true she was sacked by Twentieth Century Fox for absenteeism, the studio had subsequently reinstated her to the set of the same film at a much greater salary than the one she was on when they fired her – one version says that it was three times bigger. As a result of this triumph, she had just gone out and bought herself an entirely new wardrobe. And Dr. Greenson was weaning her off her course of drugs, with notable success.

The ink on the coroner's announcement was scarcely dry before awkward questions began to be asked. Sergeant Jack Clemmons, of the Los Angeles police department, was the first officer to arrive on the scene, at 4.30. a.m. He was told that Marilyn had been dead for about three hours, but as an experienced homicide officer it was clear to him that she had been dead for much longer than that. In his estimation, she died at least eight hours earlier.

Rigor mortis had already set in, but more significantly, so had hypostasis. The presence of this condition, which produces a purple pallor as a result of blood settling in the lowest level of the body, suggested that the actress had been lying in the same position for many hours.

As she was face down on the bed, her back and bottom were ashen, while the front of the body was livid – a clear case of hypostasis, a condition that takes many hours to reveal itself.

Clemmons had an uneasy feeling that there were other people in Marilyn's house on Fifth Helena Drive, Hollywood, at the time of his arrival, and that they did not show themselves to him. He also thought there was a peculiar atmosphere about the place.

He would also later claim that he thought the scene had been carefully stage-managed. Overdose victims are rarely found neatly arranged with their legs together, as Marilyn's had been. In the final moments of death, they invariably suffer convulsions or violent vomiting. There was no sign of any of these things. Nor was there any evidence of a glass which might have contained water, much needed if 47 tablets had to be swallowed.

Furthermore, the post-mortem carried out by Dr. Thomas Noguchi – then a relatively junior doctor but who was later to achieve a sort of fame as "Coroner to the Stars"– failed to reveal any trace of gelatine from the Nembutal capsules. Nor was there any sign of the bright yellow dye with which the capsules are coloured – a dye certain to stain the digestive tract if taken orally.

Dr. Noguchi reported: "I found no needle marks ... But interestingly I did find evidence which might have indicated violence. On Monroe's lower left back was an area of slight ecchymosis, a dark reddish-blue bruise that results from bleeding into the tissues through injury. The colour of the bruise indicated that it was fresh rather than old.

"I found absolutely no visual evidence of pills in the stomach or the small intestine. No residue. No refractile crystals. Yet the evidence of the pill bottles showed that Monroe had swallowed forty to fifty Nembutals and a large number of chloral hydrate pills."

So if Marilyn died from a drug overdose – and everyone agreed that was what she did die of – she must have taken the drug in the form of a suppository or as an injection.

According to Dr. Noguchi, there was no sign of a suppository. But he had noted the fresh bruise on the top of her left hip, a typical injection site. As there wasn't a syringe in sight, this raised the suspicion that someone else had given her the fatal jab.

To make absolutely sure that his report was accurate, Dr. Noguchi sent Marilyn's liver, together with some blood samples, to the toxicology lab for alcohol and barbiturate examination. He also forwarded some other organs, including, most importantly, the stomach and its contents, and the intestine, for "further toxicological study."

What Dr. Noguchi wrote about this very much later is interesting:

"I instantly noted that the lab technicians had not tested the other organs I had sent them. They had examined only the blood and the liver.

"Why this failure to perform all the tests, which is a routine procedure in the department today? The evidence found in the analysis of the blood and the liver, together with the empty bottle of Nembutal and the partly empty (forty pills missing out of fifty) bottle of chloral hydrate, pointed so overwhelmingly to suicide that the head toxicologist apparently felt there was no need to test any further. Specifically the blood test showed 8.0 mg% of choral hydrate, and the liver showed 13.0 mg% of pentobarbital (Nembutal), both well above fatal dosages.

"Still, I should have insisted that all the organs, including the contents of the stomach, and segments of the intestine, be analysed. But I didn't follow through as I should have. As a junior member of the staff I didn't feel I could challenge the department heads on procedures."

A few weeks later he asked the head toxicologist if he had stored the other organs of Marilyn's body that had been sent to him. He was told: "I'm sorry, but I disposed of them because we had closed the case."

We may understand why Dr. Noguchi might at this stage have been shaking his head with some concern when we learn that the two places which would have produced evidence that Marilyn had swallowed those pills that night were the stomach and intestinal tract, because they would have revealed remnants of the pills' gelatine capsules and traces of the dye which colours them.

So here was a woman who died of a massive drug overdose yet whose body revealed no evidence of drug ingestion. This was the first important contradiction in the death of Marilyn Monroe.

Another contradiction, many people thought, was her nudity, an anomaly partly because it was a chilly night, partly because overdose victims normally plan to look their best when found the following day. But if someone else had injected her, leaving that bruise on her thigh, they may first have removed her night-dress, which would have impeded them.

At the time of her death that August weekend in 1962 few people had any idea that the Kennedy brothers – President John F. and Attorney General Bobby – were the keyholders to the tragedy. Those who voted in favour of suicide declared that it was the Kennedys' rejection of Marilyn which had paved the way for her depression and death. She felt strongly that they had used her to gratify their sexual needs, then cast her aside.

She was the pin-up of a multitude of men, and John Kennedy was no exception. In 1954, when undergoing back surgery, he pinned her picture on the wall of his hospital ward. She was wearing shorts and standing with her legs wide apart. Kennedy pinned the picture upside down, so that her legs pointed towards the ceiling.

Soon after that they were introduced to one another by Frank Sinatra, a mutual friend. A friendship developed into an affair and they were sleeping together frequently during the presidential election campaign of 1960.

Winning the presidency did nothing to cool Kennedy's ardour. On the contrary, the risk appeared to add spice to the affair. The most famous blonde in the world was smuggled into his suite at New York's Carlyle Hotel. She was even smuggled on to the presidential plane, Air Force One, disguised in a black wig and sunglasses.

Actor Peter Lawford, brother-in-law to the Kennedys (he was married to their sister Pat) took a series of pictures of the actress and the President in the bath at his beach house in Malibu. The Kennedy brothers were such frequent visitors there that aides dubbed it the Pacific White House.

Such escapades would have been hazardous at any time, but Marilyn's troubled state of mind now made them doubly so. She was constantly swinging from elated heights to dark despair, a see-sawing condition fuelled by a regular intake of medicinal drugs. No public figure, let alone the President of the United States with an image to protect, should have dared to get involved with her.

She was not famed for her discretion, either. One of her closest friends was her masseur, Ralph Roberts. He once asked her innocently enough whether she had enjoyed meeting John Kennedy the day before. "Oh, yes," she replied, "and I did his back a power of good."

Years after her death, one of JFK's bodyguards told a story on British TV to the effect that Marilyn had expressed to him her disappointment about her first sex session with the President. JFK, she said, quickly undressed, dived on her, had sex and got dressed again. "She told me there was absolutely no foreplay and she was bitterly upset about that," the bodyguard recalled.

For the enemies of the Kennedy clan, who were numerous, such opportunities were too good to miss. One enemy, J. Edgar Hoover, boss of the FBI, was a law unto himself, and that bothered both JFK and Bobby. When they decided to fire him they were unaware just how much dirt the FBI had already amassed on the Kennedys.

The two brothers met Hoover in a restaurant and handed him a sealed envelope, in which it has been reported was Hoover's notice to quit. Without opening it, Hoover handed another envelope back to them. Bobby Kennedy opened it, blanched, and retired to the men's room. There was no more talk of sacking Hoover after that.

The FBI knew all about JFK's sexual activities because they had bugged the Lawford home on Malibu Beach – they knew that Marilyn Monroe, among others, had been sporting in the bath with the President.

Two other sworn enemies, Jimmy Hoffa, president of the corrupt Teamsters' Union, and Sam Giancana, Chicago's Mafia don, also used bugging techniques to build up a file on the Kennedys. In their case they bugged Marilyn's home.

Both Hoffa and Giancana had strong personal reasons for wanting to bring down the Kennedys. Both were into organised crime with the Mob, and when Bobby Kennedy became Attorney General he waged unrelenting war on organised crime, hassling Hoffa into corners, having him arrested on small issues when he was unable to pin him down on big ones, and generally making the union boss's life hard. No one had any doubts that the two men hated each other, an animosity that eventually led to Bobby Kennedy's death.

But Hoffa knew the law, too. Twice he had Bobby Kennedy thrown out of his office when the Attorney General came to arrest him. Hoffa's lawyer, William

Buffalino, confirmed Hoffa's part in the bugging surveillance during an interview long after the mobster's death. It was certainly well known to Bobby Kennedy while Hoffa was still alive, for the Attorney General carried an anti-bugging device in his briefcase.

On May 19th, 1962, three months before she died, Marilyn Monroe left the set of *Something's Got to Give* – against the wishes of the director George Cukor – to appear at John F. Kennedy's 45th birthday celebrations in New York's Madison Square Garden. She was wearing a white skin-tight dress that left little to the imagination, and she proceeded to sing her sexy version of "Happy Birthday, Mr. President."

Her appearance was arranged by Peter Lawford in his role as master of ceremonies and it brought the house down. Even Jackie Kennedy smiled wanly.

That night the president and the showgirl slept together for the last time. Even the adventurous JFK had come to realise that Marilyn was a luxury he just couldn't afford, one risk too many.

Peter Lawford, as a friend or relative of all the three main principals, is perhaps the best source for the events that followed. He spoke about these with surprising candour shortly before his own death.

"Marilyn just wouldn't accept that the affair was over," he said. "Back on the West Coast, she plunged into black despair, losing herself in drugs and barbiturates. Then she began writing these rather pathetic letters to Jack and continued to call him at the White House. She threatened to go to the press.

"He finally sent Bobby out to California to cool her off. It wasn't Bobby's intention but they became lovers and spent the night in our guesthouse room. Almost immediately the affair got very heavy, and soon Marilyn was saying she was in love with Bobby and that he had promised to marry her. It was as though she could no longer tell the difference between Bobby and Jack."

On June 27th, 1962, Bobby arrived at Marilyn's house

unaware of the fact that it was bugged by the Mafia and under surveillance by the FBI.

A memo from a Los Angeles FBI agent, William Simon, landed on Hoover's desk within days, detailing all that the Attorney General had been up to in the Malibu beach house. Now sensing danger, Bobby tried to distance himself from Marilyn. But it was too late.

On the brink of a nervous breakdown, she bombarded the Attorney General's office to no avail. He gave strict instructions that no calls from the actress should be put through to him.

She appears to have genuinely believed that she was going to marry Bobby. She had gone on record as saying that he had told her he would divorce his wife Ethel and marry her. If he did say that it would have been utterly reckless. Bobby Kennedy was a strict Catholic and as Attorney General he was upholding family values across the States. To have divorced his wife and married Marilyn Monroe would have brought him down, and the President too, for Jack was his brother and had put him in office.

Peter Lawford, in the role of peacemaker, then invited her to a dinner party on August 4th with the promise that Bobby would be there too. He did this in the hope that there could be some sort of reconciliation. As camouflage, she would be escorted by her masseur, Ralph Roberts.

Marilyn at first accepted, then changed her mind and refused to go. Suddenly, it seemed that she was giving up on the idea of romance with the Kennedys. She did not want to see Bobby Kennedy any more, although it was to transpire that Bobby, worried about whether she might go public on their affair, now desperately wanted to see her to make sure that everything was all right.

That was the scenario leading up to Marilyn's final day, Saturday, August 4th. She got up early, which was unusual, complaining that she had slept badly. Her close friend, Pat Newcomb, who had spent that night in the guest's room, said Marilyn was moody in the morning, but nothing more than moody.

What is certain is that twice that day Bobby Kennedy, who was week-ending in California, called at Marilyn's house – he was seen going in by neighbours. Tapes produced from the bugging equipment seem to suggest that he arrived with other people; that there was a terrible row between him and Marilyn, and that he was looking for a red book in which she kept addresses. She did not let him have the book, and it has never been found.

Indeed, a report by the district attorney on the death of Marilyn wondered whether the red book, or diary as it was called, ever existed, despite the fact that it was seen in Marilyn's possession by at least three people.

It was also seen by an assistant in the coroner's office, a young man named Lionel Grandison. His role in the affair of the red book is revealed in a special inquiry report which was designed to re-open the case in 1982 – twenty years after Marilyn's death:

"Mr. Grandison reported that he saw associated with Miss Monroe's property a scrawled note and a red diary. He alleges that both items disappeared from the coroner's office shortly after the post-mortem was performed. Grandison claims to have briefly examined the diary and noted that it contained the names of government figures and perhaps matters relating to sensitive government operations. Our investigation points to the conclusion that Mr. Grandison is in error."

The red book, remember, was the purpose of at least one visit, probably both visits, of Robert Kennedy that Saturday to Fifth Helena Drive, and the object of his frantic search of the house.

Did it exist? Jeanne Carmen, a close friend of Marilyn's, had no doubt that it did. She remembered that one day she was at Marilyn's when Robert Kennedy called. He found the red book, read its contents and became very angry, throwing it across the room and shouting, "Get rid of this!"

But according to the DA's report, anyone who saw that red book was in error, because there was no red book.

On her last night alive Marilyn went to bed at 8 p.m., taking one of her telephones and making calls to friends. In the absence of solid facts, the theories about her death that night have been many and varied.

Sam Giancana's half-brother, Chuck, claimed in 1992 that Giancana murdered Marilyn by means of a suppository filled with drugs. He said: "Sam believed that by murdering Marilyn, Bobby Kennedy's affair with her would be exposed. Then it might be possible to depose the rulers of Camelot."

Camelot, the court of King Arthur and the Knights of the Round Table, was adopted as a name by Kennedy admirers to describe the new political regime.

Giancana killed Marilyn, it was claimed, at the instigation of the CIA. The CIA were aware that the Kennedys had told Marilyn a few things about them, and were fearful of exposure by her. The CIA's bosses also had good reason to hate the Kennedys, for after the Cuban Bay of Pigs debacle, which was master-minded by the CIA, John Kennedy had vowed to disband the entire organisation. CIA involvement in Marilyn's death, it was suggested, occurred because they hoped it would expose the Kennedy liaison with her and thereby discredit the President.

Four professional killers are supposed to have entered her house some time before midnight, taped her mouth and killed her by introducing the suppository containing a cocktail of barbiturates and chloral hydrate.

It is unlikely, however, that a suppository could have contained the lethal dose that killed Marilyn. It is also an unlikely method for a Mafia killing – there were at least half a dozen simpler ways of killing her. Even so, murder theorists can be reasonably comfortable with this idea, for if murder is to be committed with no marks left on the body, the best point of entry for such a killing is the rectum.

Ten years before Chuck Giancana's book, Milo Speriglio, a private detective hired by Marilyn's friend Robert Slazer, came up with an equally startling claim.

Aware that Marilyn's home had been bugged by the Mafia, he made a deal with a secret informer who had acquired some of the tapes, including one which bore the sounds of Marilyn's last movements.

According to Speriglio, his informant played this over the phone to him. At first, he said, a woman was heard being slapped around. Then there was a thud, like a body hitting the floor, followed by more cries, although these were muffled.

Later a man's voice asked, "What are we going to do with the body?" Speriglio said he recognised the voices of the two men. One was a top politician and the other was a film star, but he didn't name them.

This story should be considered with some caution, however. "A woman being slapped around," and "A thud, like a body hitting the floor," would be difficult sounds to distinguish over a bugging device, given, as we have already seen, the thickness of Marilyn's bedroom carpet. A top politician and a film star could mean only two things – presumably they were not identified by name because of the unreliability of the tape sounds.

There was also a fairly widespread theory about a faked suicide plot that went drastically wrong. The central figure in this was someone who had once been close to both the Kennedys and Marilyn. Like the actress, this person felt he had been badly betrayed by the clan and wanted vengeance.

So the two of them planned a fake suicide bid that would alert the press of the world and thus give Marilyn the chance to tell the story that would destroy the Kennedys. Only the fake became all too real.

If this were true, it would at least explain Marilyn's curious enquiry of her housekeeper, Eunice Murray, on the morning of Saturday, August 4th, her last day alive, when she asked: "Is there any oxygen around?" Oxygen is used to help save victims of barbiturate overdose.

It was an absurd question, one that continues to mystify. Private homes in Hollywood do not normally contain oxygen, and Marilyn must have known better than anyone that there was none around, since she owned the house. Which begs the question, did she ever ask about oxygen in the first place? For Eunice Murray turned out to be an unreliable witness who regularly changed her story about what happened that night and indeed was still changing it 20 years after Marilyn's death.

FBI chief Hoover had his own theory. Years later he responded to a question about the case from a young Washington neighbour, Anthony Calomaris, by saying flatly, "She was murdered. The Kennedys were involved."

But surely the most knowledgeable voice in all this has to be that of Peter Lawford, the one member of the inner quartet (Marilyn, John and Bobby Kennedy being the others) to survive into the 1980s.

It was then that he admitted that Bobby Kennedy flew into Los Angeles on August 4th for the express purpose of having a showdown with Marilyn. Officially he had come to California to address the American Bar Association and to take a brief holiday with his family.

With Lawford alongside, he went to Marilyn's house, where there was an angry quarrel. "Marilyn," said Lawford, "disclosed how first thing Monday morning she was going to call a press conference and tell the world about the treatment she had suffered at the hands of the Kennedy brothers.

"Bobby became livid. In no uncertain terms he told her she was going to have to leave both Jack and himself alone ... no more telephone calls, no letters, nothing."

Then, according to Lawford, the row ended with Marilyn hysterical and having to be subdued. Her psychiatrist, Dr. Greenson, was called to the house, and he talked quietly to her. Eventually, believing she was now calm, he went off to dinner with his wife.

The most dangerous thing about this was Marilyn's threat to call a press conference and spill the beans. That would have spelled curtains for the Kennedys, from the President down to the most junior member of the family.

Marilyn Monroe frequently called press conferences and any number of journalists turned up in the hope of extracting some morsel from the Hollywood pie.

On Monday, August 6th, they would have gone off with the whole pie itself.

But would she have carried out her threat in the cold light of that Monday morning? For Marilyn Monroe was no fool. She would have known that if she told all about herself and the Kennedys it would be the end of her own career as well. No one would employ her after such an event.

Round about seven o'clock that Saturday evening of her death – which was probably about half an hour after Bobby Kennedy's last visit to her house – Marilyn spoke to her stepson, Joe DiMaggio Junior, on the phone. He was to say later that she was happy and joked with him for quite a while.

If this is true, she had clearly recovered her composure after the row with Kennedy, and reconciled herself to having lost her attempt to gain possession of him. Either that or she was putting a brave face on things for her stepson, and not letting her troubles overlap on to him.

Lawford was still hoping that she would turn up at the restaurant where he and Bobby Kennedy and Kennedy's family were having dinner that night. When she hadn't arrived by eight o'clock Lawford rang to say, "Hey, Charlie [Charlie was a form of greeting in vogue in the 1960s], what happened to you?"

According to Lawford, she said she was too tired to come. Her voice sounded slurred, as though she had been drinking, or was drugged. Then she said, "Say goodbye to Pat [Lawford's wife], and say goodbye to the President and say goodbye to yourself, because you're such a nice guy."

There was an air of finality about this which set all the alarm bells ringing for Lawford. Fearing that she had suicide in mind, he phoned his manager from the restaurant and asked him to call and check up on the actress. The manager was reluctant to become involved and strongly advised Lawford to stay clear too. "You're the brother-in-law of the President of the United States," he reminded him. "Just think of the scandal this would cause."

But subsequent evidence gathered from police officers, from Marilyn's psychiatrist, ambulancemen and doctors suggests that Lawford failed to follow that advice; that instead he returned to the actress's home with Bobby Kennedy to find Marilyn either dead or dying.

According to this theory, they then phoned for an ambulance. Half-way to the hospital they realised that Marilyn was dead, so they ordered the ambulance to do an about-turn back to Marilyn's house. They then had the body replaced on the bed – hence it was found in a position inconsistent with death by drug overdose – and Bobby Kennedy left Los Angeles in a hurry the way he had arrived, by helicopter and private plane.

This theory at least has the merit of neatly fitting the known facts. Dr. Greenson confirmed privately years later that Bobby Kennedy was in the house that night, and also that an ambulance was called. Neighbours in Fifth Helena Drive also confirmed that an ambulance was standing in the driveway that night.

But no ambulance was ever called, according to Walt Schaefer , the owner of the ambulance company which was alleged to have sent a vehicle to Fifth Helena Drive. At least, that was his first story. Twenty years later, when the district attorney held his new inquiry, Schaefer remembered that an ambulance was called. The driver's name was Ken Hunter.

According to Hunter, who also now spoke readily of the incident, when he and his partner arrived at Marilyn's house she was dead. No, Schaefer now recalled, she wasn't dead, she was still alive, and the ambulance took her to Santa Monica Hospital.

Hunter claimed that his ambulance partner that night was Murray Liebowitz, but Liebowitz insisted he wasn't, because he was not on duty that night. But another of

Schaefer's ambulancemen, James Hall, also claimed that he was the driver that night, and that his partner wasn't Hunter but Liebowitz.

James Hall remembered a good deal more. He recalled arriving around 3.30 a.m., and seeing Pat Newcomb, Marilyn's friend, who was weeping and crying out, "She's dead!" Marilyn was in the guest room and she was still alive.

Hall said he tried mouth-to-mouth resuscitation to good effect, but then someone arrived who said he was Marilyn's doctor. The newcomer, who Hall later identified as Dr. Ralph Greenson, took over from him, tried to revive her, and when he was unsuccessful produced from his bag a hypodermic with the needle in place, and injected her so roughly that "there was a snap," as if the needle had broken. Within a minute she was dead.

This bizarre story hardly stands up. Dr. Hyman Engelberg, Marilyn's doctor, as distinct from Greenson, who was her psychiatrist, was in the house at the time and would not have allowed the sequence of events that Hall said took place. Besides being a psychiatrist, Greenson was also a qualified medical doctor, but it is scarcely believable that a doctor would take a hypodermic out of his bag with the needle already fitted and jab it into his patient so hard that it broke.

The implied suggestion, of course, is that Hall watched Marilyn being murdered by her own psychiatrist, which has to be dismissed. But what cannot be dismissed is that an ambulance did arrive at Marilyn's house and for some reason its presence there was covered up.

Nothing more can be determined about the ambulance because Walter Schaefer subsequently destroyed his old records, as did the Santa Monica Hospital.

If the Mafia had hoped to use the Monroe connection to bring down the Kennedys, they were to be disappointed. Hoover and the FBI out-manoeuvred them all the way down the line.

Like the ambulance records and the hospital records,

the records of Marilyn's phone calls simply disappeared, in the same way that her red book, in which were listed the private numbers of the Kennedys and also one or two mobsters, disappeared. Long before the police arrived at Marilyn's house the place was "swept" of all its documents and files.

Most remarkable of all in a free press, it is today impossible to find a single still picture of Marilyn with either of the Kennedys. Globe Photos did have two close-ups of John F. Kennedy and Marilyn at that very public birthday party in Madison Square Garden. But a fortnight after the star's death, two burly fellows visited Globe's offices and took away both the pictures and the negatives. They said they were from the FBI, and they had the badges to prove it.

Yet another interesting theory in the case was published five years ago by the investigative journalist Matthew Smith, who argued in *The Men who Killed Marilyn* (Bloomsbury, 1996) that she was undoubtedly murdered, first because of the absence of drugs in her stomach when the post-mortem was carried out, and second because of the huge volume of drugs found in her body.

These were enough to kill several people, and if taken by the mouth would have killed her long before she had had enough to account for the entire drug content of her body. So the only logical conclusion, says Smith, was that the drugs were injected by enema.

The theory is that shortly after speaking on the phone to a friend at about ten o'clock, Marilyn was attacked in her bedroom. At that time Mrs. Murray had gone off to bed. The attackers gave Marilyn some kind of anaesthetic, carried her to the guest room, farthest away from any other rooms in the house, stripped her and administered an enema containing lethal drugs in liquid form while she was still unconscious. All this would have taken no more than about 15 minutes.

For this the killers must have had an intimate knowledge of the layout of the house. They would have known that

Marilyn occasionally used enemas as part of her beauty treatment, and they would have known the kind of drugs she was regularly taking.

At some time after the attack Mrs. Murray, probably disturbed by the sound of the killers, went into Marilyn's room and found it empty. She searched the house and found her employer in the guest room. She called a doctor, failed to get through at first and finally Dr. Greenson arrived shortly after midnight, when Marilyn was already dead.

But between the murder and the doctor's arrival the ambulance had been called by someone unknown, and it arrived shortly before midnight. On the way to Santa Monica Hospital the ambulancemen were aware that they had a corpse on board, so the body was returned to Fifth Helena Drive without ever going to the hospital.

Someone else arrived at the house before the police – the publicist Arthur Jacobs, who had received an urgent call at the Hollywood Bowl concert around 10.30 that night. His time of arrival was 11 p.m. His job was to protect his client's image. He was also aware that the political fate of the Attorney General, and through him the President, might depend on the story he put out to the media and his handling of it.

The decision to promote the idea of accidental suicide, says Matthew Smith, provided the key to covering the killers' tracks. This gave the police the opportunity to play the tragedy down, "conducting, overtly, a routine enquiry into a straightforward suicide, and effectively disallowing the in-depth investigation which would have been necessary had any suggestion of homicide been raised."

The death of Marilyn Monroe failed in its objective to bring down the Kennedys. But the assailants refused to give up – they simply went out and killed the Kennedys as well.

2

GIANNI VERSACE
Madman's Strike—or Mafia Hit?

Like many another very wealthy man, the internationally renowned fashion designer Gianni Versace took pleasure in simple everyday things. He enjoyed his regular morning stroll to buy an Italian newspaper and have breakfast at the News Cafe just down the road from his $3 million Miami home.

And as far as that went, July 15th, 1997, was like any other day. He was up at 8 a.m. and half an hour later he set out as usual from his Spanish-style mansion, "Casa Casuarina" on Ocean Drive, dressed casually in a shirt, shorts and flip-flop sandals. After a breakfast of coffee and fruit juice at the cafe he remarked to the proprietor, "It's a beautiful day."

But for Gianni Versace and his horrified neighbours what had begun as a beautiful day was soon to become a tragic one. It was just before 9 a.m. when he arrived back at Casa Casuarina. As he unlocked the ornate wrought-iron gates a young man wearing soft-soled trainers crept up behind him and pulled a pistol from behind his back. He pressed the muzzle against Versace's head and shouted some curses in Italian. Then he fired twice.

The fashion designer fell, rolling down his white marble steps to end sprawling on the pavement, leaving a trail of blood behind him. His sandals lay forlornly on the steps with the blood-spattered Italian newspaper. Weirdly, a dead pigeon lay beside his body.

The cold-blooded assassin walked calmly away to where a yellow taxi was parked on Ocean Drive, its lights blinking as if signalling. Witnesses were to describe the man as white, in his mid-twenties, wearing a white top, black shorts and baseball cap.

Within three minutes an ambulance was on the scene and Versace was rushed to the nearby Jackson Memorial Hospital. He was dead on arrival.

Aged 50, Versace was at the peak of his career, designing clothes for the world's very rich and very famous. He had recently extended his huge fashion empire with the opening of a branch in London's Old Bond Street, decked-out like a Roman villa.

His business was valued at close to a billion dollars and his personal fortune was estimated to be around $400 million. In addition to his Miami home he had two other equally luxurious retreats, in New York and Milan, as well as a villa on the shore of Lake Como.

But the villa on Miami's Ocean Drive was his favourite. He shared it with his long-term lover Antonio D'Amico, making no secret of his homosexuality. It had been rumoured that he was dying of AIDS, but it was a fact that he had beaten cancer of the neck three years previously, and his tumour was in remission.

Friends with homes nearby – stars like Madonna, Sylvester Stallone and Gloria Estefan – had advised him to hire security guards, but Versace refused. He valued his privacy too much for that, he told them.

The police were puzzled by the lack of an apparent motive for his murder. No attempt had been made to rob him, so was he the victim of a Mafia execution or had he been killed by an embittered former lover?

Miami's Police Chief, Richard Barreto, addressed a hastily convened press conference. He announced that although investigators were not ruling out a lovers' quarrel or a business feud, he believed that Versace had been executed by a killer who had stalked him, possibly for weeks.

"This was a hit," he said. "We do know that it was not a random act of violence... I believe he was targeted."

This prompted immediate speculation about Mafia involvement. It was not the first time that allegations had been made about a link between the Versace empire and organised crime. It was common knowledge that the Mafia had controlled the clothing industry in New York and other cities for many years, although there was little evidence that they had penetrated the world of haute couture.

The fashion designer had acknowledged in an interview two years earlier that rumours linked the Versace parent company in Italy with laundering drugs money for the Mob. He said indignantly: "They even say I am a Mafioso. That can hurt you. That can hurt your family values."

He denied all such claims, but many in the fashion world had secret doubts about whether Versace had been able to escape the tentacles of the Mob.

The police knew that if this were a contract killing it would be a difficult one to crack, for no better reason than that Florida suffers an incredible 200 to 300 contract slayings a year, so well planned that half of them go unsolved.

And there was hardly a proliferation of clues in this case. A few clothes similar to those worn by the killer were found abandoned, along with a backpack, in an underground car park nearby. That suggested that the gunman had gone to a vehicle after shooting Versace, and changed his clothing.

Some witnesses thought they saw Versace greet the assassin. Had they known one another? The police also looked into a disturbance which had taken place outside the designer's home a few nights before his murder.

Inevitably as they probed deeper for any pointers to the killer, the seamier side of the victim's life came in for close scrutiny. And Versace's private life was not that clean for detectives seeking a possible Mafia link. His elder brother was convicted in the early 1990s of bribing tax inspectors in Italy and was heavily fined and given a 14-month suspended jail sentence. Gianni Versace himself had been under investigation for possible tax evasion.

But all such theories rapidly dissolved when the FBI were called in and almost instantly linked the murder to a young gay serial killer who had been on their "Ten Most Wanted" list since June 12th. The suspect was Andrew Philip Cunanan, wanted for questioning about four recent murders.

Cunanan's story was depressingly symptomatic of our times. It was believed that he was systematically killing ex-lovers after being diagnosed HIV positive. So was Gianni Versace an ex-lover, and was he HIV positive too?

An FBI spokesman didn't know the answer to that one. But he did say that the description of the killer given by witnesses fitted Cunanan to a tee.

"Cunanan is a one-man killing machine, armed and very, very dangerous," the spokesman said. "He supports himself by dating older homosexuals who shower him with gifts and cash in exchange for sex and affection."

The FBI knew all about Andrew Cunanan. They knew that as a youth he had appeared to be a typical all-American teenager, if a little more handsome than most. His Filipino origins gave him a certain exotic charm, and he was blessed with a firm, lean body with a skin-colour that required no tanning. He gleamed bronze on the beach and the heavy gold Virgin Mary medallion which hung around his neck glinted in the sun.

Cunanan went to Bishop's High School in La Jolla, San Diego, where he was an exceptional student – voted by his classmates as the student least likely to be forgotten. Forever an extrovert, he went to the traditional high school dance wearing a red leather jump-suit, and he made no attempt to hide the fact that he was gay.

It was traditional for students to produce a year-book in their graduation year, with their photographs and little personal notes beneath, such as: "I intend to become a great doctor." Ominously, the 18-year-old Cunanan put beneath his picture the prophetic words uttered by King Louis XV of France: "*Après moi, le déluge*" – "After me, there will be disaster."

Cunanan left school and enjoyed a comfortable middle-class life-style. Relatives remembered his acute intelligence, his precociousness and the taste for luxury he demonstrated from an early age. They remembered especially how he was indulged by his fond parents, who gave him a sports car for his 16th birthday.

The youngest of four children, he was born in a tiny house in a shanty town in the Philippines. They were dirt-poor. Somehow the family managed to emigrate to San Diego, California, where Cunanan's father, Modesto, set up in business as a stockbroker. He was successful at first, and the family lived in relative comfort. They were devout Roman Catholics – Andrew Cunanan's mother was proud to say that her son had read the Bible studiously since the age of six.

Suddenly the Cunanan family's life collapsed around them. Following a financial scandal, Modesto Cunanan fled the country, leaving his wife and children penniless. In due time Andrew Cunanan followed him back to the Philippines.

He was later to claim that his father severely ill-treated him as a child – "he beat me black and blue," he told a friend. Some think he was traumatised by his family's break-up, others think he was just a spoilt brat with an inventive line of patter. Eventually he returned to San Diego where his relatives lived – he was particularly close to his elderly aunt Barbara – and tried to pick up the threads of his life.

But that was to prove much harder than Cunanan imagined. For he was having to come to terms with the darker side of his life – he was sexually ambivalent. He liked girls but he was also attracted to men. He also liked his sex rough and was into bondage and sado-masochism.

In 1992 he met a Spanish woman in a bar and married

her. His close friend Georgi Kalamaras said of the encounter: "Andrew married this girl to help her get a green card to stay in the US. But he fell in love with her."

At the time of the hasty wedding Cunanan was the tomboy lover of an elderly millionaire businessman. Kalamaras said: "He found himself in a real dilemma. This man was paying him an allowance of two thousand dollars a month and had given him a sports car. He couldn't break the relationship – he was completely tied down."

Cunanan's troubles multiplied when his wife told him she was pregnant. The announcement devastated him – although according to Kalamaras he eventually "started to come round to the idea." One day Cunanan broke down at his friend's house and told him that the pressure of leading a double life was destroying him.

"He seemed to be at breaking point," Kalamaras remembered. "But he knew that if the money stopped coming in they'd all be in trouble."

Cunanan began peddling drugs, made some money, but also ran up huge debts because of his liking for expensive clothes and the flashiest car on the market. When the financial pressure really began to hurt he turned to prostitution, selling himself to older men. And sometimes women. He became a gay gigolo.

On the gay scene in San Diego and San Francisco in the late 1980s he styled himself Andrew DeSilva, and claimed to be a Hollywood chief executive with a Riviera mansion. At other times he would present himself as Lieutenant-Commander Cummings, a Yale-educated importer of antiques.

Cunanan was a hedonist by nature, a playboy masking his deep insecurity by pretending to be someone else. Now in his mid-twenties he had become a party animal with kinky tastes, well-known in the gay communities of several West Coast cities. He loved to be the great pretender, forever bragging about his education, his breeding, and the big jobs he had held down. Sometimes he claimed to be the son of a wealthy Filipino plantation-owner.

One day in the midst of these play-acting years Cunanan let it be known that he had met the Italian fashion designer Gianni Versace at the San Francisco Opera House in 1990. That seemed to be the start of a Versace obsession. After that he was always dropping Versace's name at parties, and invariably wore the designer's own label underwear.

In the evenings he cruised the trendy gay bars and his public manner was fun-loving and generous. In private he indulged his sado-masochism, regularly adding to his burgeoning collection of videos depicting brutal sex-torture scenes.

Cunanan craved attention, and thought he wasn't getting the recognition he deserved. He thought perhaps he should have been a film star by now, because he next developed an obsession for Tom Cruise, turning his bedroom into a virtual shrine to him, with photographs of the actor all over the walls.

But about this time his own looks started to fade and the good living was adding unsightly weight to the once-taut body. Cunanan became almost pudgy, his weight, fuelled by a heavy intake of vodka, ballooning to nearly 15 stone. The money began to dry up and the rent boy began to realise he would never become another Tom Cruise.

Cunanan was at his wits' end when lack of cash forced him to sell his car and move home to a tiny studio flat. Friends he spoke to at this time remembered him being tired and despondent. But suddenly his luck seemed to change. He let it be known that he was into a new and "perfect" relationship with a new man, a wealthy architect named David Madson, 33.

Since both the partners in that relationship are now dead, it is difficult even to conjecture what went wrong. What is known was that on April 24th, 1997, Andrew Cunanan treated four of his friends to what he called a last supper at a swank San Diego restaurant. What the guests didn't know is that despite any financial help that Cunanan was receiving from David Madson, the limit on his credit card, with which he paid the bill, was nearly up.

At the end of the meal he told his guests rather melodramatically: "I will be leaving town tomorrow to take care of some business. Everyone has their own version of what they really think I am. But no one knows the real truth."

The following day he flew out of San Diego for Minneapolis, where he was picked up at the airport by David Madson. What happened in the next few days can only be pieced together by taking all the facts into consideration.

Cunanan, it is believed, had arrived in Minneapolis on a vengeance mission, believing he had contracted AIDS from one of his sexual partners. The once-normal teenager living the American dream was about to become a monster, on a mission of slaughter across the United States.

It is known that one of his former lovers in San Diego was 28-year-old ex-navy Lieutenant Jeffrey Trail, who had moved to Minneapolis to become the manager of a gas company. It is known, too, that the break-up in their relationship had upset Cunanan. The first "business" he had told friends he was about to take care of probably concerns the murder of Jeffrey Trail, and suggests that he may have made the journey to Minneapolis with feelings of rage, rejection and despair.

Almost certainly Cunanan stayed at Madson's apartment. Shortly after his arrival there he went to Minnesota, contacted Jeffrey Trail, and later invited him to come and visit him at Madson's apartment, claiming perhaps to be the owner. The invitation was discovered by the police, who found a message from Cunanan on Trail's answering machine, suggesting that Trail come over for a meal.

Trail accepted the invitation and arrived at the apartment on April 29th. There his former friend Cunanan bludgeoned him to death with a claw hammer, rolled up his body in a carpet and put it in a locked cupboard.

When David Madson returned home that evening he found Cunanan waiting for him. Detectives believe that Cunanan held Madson hostage for about two days while Trail's body slowly rotted in the cupboard.

On May 3rd – five days after the murder of Jeffrey Trail – Madson's body was found by fishermen in a lake about 30 miles north of Minneapolis. He had been shot in the back of the head, hit-man style, and had been dead for a day. When police identified the body they searched Madson's apartment and discovered the corpse of Jeffrey Trail.

They also found a nylon bag with Cunanan's name tag on it. Inside the bag was a box of Golden Saber bullets of the type used to kill David Madson. Ten bullets were missing from the box.

One thing that was evident was that Cunanan was making no attempt to cover his actions – he was leaving clues as in a paper-chase. He was either being arrogant, daring the police to catch him, or stupid, or he simply didn't care.

At this point the police weren't exactly sure what was happening. Had David Madson killed Jeffrey Trail and then been killed himself? They figured it out and finally decided that Cunanan had first killed Trail with the claw hammer. The killer and David Madson then remained in the apartment until they drove out to the lake where Cunanan shot Madson with Trail's .40 calibre pistol.

What they were sure of, though, was that Madson's red Cherokee Jeep was missing. They issued a red alert for the vehicle.

They were to pursue Cunanan from Minnesota to Chicago and finally to Miami, but all the time he eluded them. In the motel rooms he rented during his flight they found sado-masochistic videos under the beds, a transvestite wardrobe and leather thongs for binding victims.

The man they wanted for questioning was not only highly dangerous, but into just about everything he could be into.

As the hunt for Andrew Cunanan hotted up, on May 4th a 72-year-old millionaire property developer named Lee Miglin was found dead by his wife in the garage of their home in the wealthy "Gold Coast" suburb of Chicago. Miglan had been slowly and brutally murdered.

Was there a connection with the fugitive Cunanan? Lee Miglin, it was thought, might have been the father of one of Cunanan's former lovers. He had a son who was an actor.

Lee Miglin was tortured for hours before his throat was cut with a saw and his chest stabbed with pruning shears. His head was bound with masking tape, leaving just a small hole for his nostrils, allowing him to breathe.

His body, wrapped in brown plastic, was riddled with small wounds. When the tape was removed it was discovered that his face had been gouged. His chest was crushed where his car had been driven over him six or seven times.

The killer had let himself into Miglin's house with a pass-key, remaining there overnight, making himself a sandwich and having a shave before driving off in his victim's car after stealing $2,000 and several suits.

Police described the killing as a "torture murder." There was evidence that Cunanan had re-enacted a scene from a porn video. Chicago County Sheriff Randy Schwegman said: "It was the sickest movie I had ever seen. It sent a chill up my spine. He'd copied a scene in it virtually identically... This man will not stop killing. What does he have to lose? He's like a mad dog running through the countryside."

David Madson's missing red Jeep was found near the Miglin house, while Miglin's green 1994 Lexus car was missing. Had Cunanan met his victim in a gay bar? Miglin's wife said that her husband had never met his killer and was not gay. Detectives speculated that Miglin might have come into contact with Cunanan by chance and was simply murdered for his car.

This seemed to be confirmed by the next killing. On May 9th the body of William Reese, a 45-year-old cemetery caretaker, was found at Finn's Point National Cemetery in Pennsville, New Jersey. Reese was shot with the same .40 calibre handgun which had killed David Madson. He was tossed into a shallow grave. Lee Miglin's green Lexus was found nearby, and Reese's 1995 red Chevrolet truck was missing.

This was the killer's signature – every serial killer has one. Cunanan stole his victim's vehicle for transport to the next killing. As nationwide murder charges were being filed against him he was now only 100 miles from his final destination. A couple of hours later Cunanan was in Miami.

He had driven all the way to Miami to kill his hero, to gain the recognition he had so long craved. He made no effort to cover his tracks and the police were later to be accused of sloppiness in their handling of the case. He left William Reese's truck – containing his own passport – in a public car park where it remained unnoticed by police for a month.

During that month – it may in fact have been as long as two months – Cunanan cruised the local gay bars, stalking his victim, checking out every movement made by Gianni Versace. He used the Normandy Plaza motel as his base. He had no cash of his own so he pawned a rare gold coin stolen from Lee Miglin, using his own name and signature and giving his motel address.

That in itself was an open invitation to the authorities to come and arrest him, because under the state laws of Florida information on rare objects which have been pawned has to be forwarded to the police within 24 hours – that would have been July 8th at the latest – a week before Versace was murdered. Cunanan's details were forwarded, but they were apparently not examined.

So, a week later, came the cold-blooded killing that shocked the world. A security camera caught an image of the murderer walking calmly away from Versace's body. It showed the image to be that of Andrew Cunanan.

The massive manhunt was led by the FBI, announcing a reward totalling $40,000 for information leading to the capture of Versace's killer. Pictures issued of Cunanan included some of him dressed as a woman. The FBI said they had reason to believe that he sometimes disguised himself. Sightings of Cunanan came in from almost every state in the Union.

Panic set in when it was thought that Cunanan had killed yet again – for the sixth time. Only 10 minutes away from the Versace crime scene on Ocean Drive, and only two days later, a man resembling Cunanan was seen running from a luxury bungalow where police later found the body of a doctor in a bedroom, his trousers around his ankles. Like Versace, the victim was gay and was shot in the head.

The dead man was 44-year-old Dr. Silvio Alfonso, born in Cuba and living alone in the exclusive Miami suburb. Detectives conjectured that he might have picked up Cunanan in a gay bar and taken him home. The murder spread waves of fear through America's gay communities and potential high-risk targets were warned to be on their guard.

The last act in the drama began to be played out before 4 p.m. on July 23rd, nine days after Versace's murder. It started with a phone call from the caretaker of a marina at Indian Creek, 40 blocks north of Versace's mansion. The caretaker reported that a man in a blue and white houseboat moored at the marina had shot at him.

Detectives rushed to the spot, suspecting that this was where Cunanan had been hiding up since he killed Versace. Police marksmen took up their positions, training high-velocity rifles on the two-storey houseboat. Helicopters circled overhead while boats, dogs, and officers threw a cordon around the area. Cunanan's last stand was about to begin.

It lasted five hours. During the tense siege police tossed a telephone on to the deck in an effort to get the trapped man to speak to them, repeatedly shouting "Pick it up!"

but Cunanan did not respond. It ended just before 8 p.m. with a muffled shot from the houseboat, followed by silence.

Had Cunanan shot himself? It was decided to take no chances and the police assault on the houseboat was in classic Hollywood style. First, concussion grenades and tear gas were fired into the boat, then eight officers in gas masks and bullet proof vests stormed the vessel.

The smoke and fumes were so dense that at first they failed to spot Andrew Cunanan lying on the bed in the master stateroom. It wasn't until an hour or so later that the police announced that they had found a body. Cunanan had put the barrel of a semi-automatic pistol into his mouth and blown half his face away. Near his hand lay the gun with which he shot Versace and two other victims. There was no suicide note.

A policeman commented: "Half his head was missing. He was unrecognisable as a human – but then he wasn't human."

Cunanan had made such a mess of his death in fact that police first had to decide whether the body was that of the fugitive. Identification was finally accomplished when a thumbprint from the corpse matched one found on the pawned coin.

Police chief Barreto announced: "The reign of terror brought upon us by Andrew Cunanan is now over. All across our nation our citizens can stand down and breathe a sigh of relief." That statement, added an FBI officer, was "the highest-ranking sigh of relief I've heard for a long while."

The police chief admitted that there were "still a lot of unanswered questions. There is still a lot of evidence being processed."

An FBI agent said there was no evidence that Cunanan knew the German owner of the houseboat. Deflecting criticism of the FBI's handling of the case, he said: "Listen, he managed to get forty blocks from the crime scene. That's the best he could do all this time. I think we did a pretty good job."

Robert Resslere, former head of the FBI's Behavioural Sciences Unit, said that serial killers were usually methodical and planned their operations meticulously. Cunanan was very untypical. He appeared to be someone spurred on by an unbearable emotional conflict.

"These kind of people go off on rampages that sometimes last days and sometimes last months. A spree killer is suicidal by his very motivation. A pure serial killer is going for the long term, and they can go on for years. What we have here is a man who sees the end coming soon and intends to go out in style."

Dr. Casey Jordan, a criminologist specialising in serial killers, commented: "He wanted attention, but he cannot have foreseen how much there would have been. He must have known there was no way out of this alive. I'm sure we will know more about this case in the coming weeks as people who knew Cunanan start to speak. Many of them were too afraid to talk while he was still alive."

Dr. Jordan was right – some of the killer's friends did start talking. Mike Scott was one of them. He said that earlier that year Cunanan was telling friends he had been given the news at a San Diego health clinic that he was HIV positive. "He appeared to be devastated."

Later Cunanan packed a bag and drove to Los Angeles, where he looked up Scott. "He turned up here kinda unexpectedly. I think he'd had a bust-up with a boy friend."

Within days the penniless gigolo was admitting to friends that he was working the notorious street corners near the transvestite prostitutes' hangout on Santa Monica Boulevard. Scott said: "Once he told me he had picked up a really well-known actor and had sex with him in his car parked in an alleyway. He joked that he may have given the guy AIDS. I was horrified."

Rumours continued to persist that Versace was killed by a Mafia hit-man, but the weapon used made this unlikely. A professional uses a smaller calibre gun, firing bullets that tumble around inside the head, scrambling the brain. A bigger calibre, like the .40 used in these killings, would have had sufficient velocity to exit the skull, and men have been known to survive with half their brains blown away. If a hit-man killed Versace, he was an inept one.

A week after the fashion designer's murder, however, the Florida Department of Law Enforcement announced that it was looking into the possibility that gangland bosses had ordered the killing. A special police task force interviewed Frank Monte, a private investigator hired the previous year by Versace. Monte believed that the killing was a result of a Mafia hit.

It was the two shots to the back of the head and the dead bird that convinced him. Songbirds are traditionally used as a signature in contract killings to symbolise the death of those who have talked too much.

Monte said: "If you shoot a guy in the back of the head and you have a dead bird on the ground, you are trying to leave a message. As far as I am concerned this was a professional hit ordered by organised criminals."

A security consultant from New York, Monte was hired by Versace to investigate the murder of a former boy friend by a former lover. At the time, Monte said, Versace had confided his fears of organised crime in the fashion world. "We had this conversation in which he said he was anxious about problems inside the business. He was worried about coming clean." When Monte asked Versace if he was talking about thousands of dollars, Versace replied bluntly, "Millions."

Monte claimed that Versace was killed because he threatened to blow the whistle on the laundering of drug profits. He was also living in fear of being kidnapped for ransom.

Fashion insiders spoke about the haunted last months of Versace. Despite beating cancer, he was losing his hair in clumps and his weight was plummeting. Friends remarked that his mood was growing sombre. An employee said that over the previous few months the boss became "a more anxious man." There were clashes with staff and he looked tired and flustered. He hotly denied Mafia links but admitted he was "at war" with his younger sister Donatella – who was to become the real power behind the Versace empire. The feisty bottle-blonde had already been installed as the firm's president.

Meanwhile Versace's ashes were flown back to Italy by private jet for a simple funeral, to be followed by a Mass in Milan Cathedral, with Diana, Princess of Wales, among the mourners, one arm around the shoulders of a sobbing Elton John.

Florida police said later that they did not believe that Andrew Cunanan remained in the houseboat ever since the murder, although he must have stayed "holed up in a very tight area." The owner of another vessel nearby had reported that a stranger slept on the deck of his boat two nights after Versace's murder.

The FBI's deputy director, William Esposito, said that after the killing the bureau made contact with a friend of Cunanan's who received a phone call from the killer. Cunanan sounded "nervous and agitated" but did not confide anything about the killing. The two men did, however, discuss "who was on the east coast who might have a passport, which Cunanan could use to flee the country."

A number of secrets died with Cunanan – not least his exact motives and what connection he might have if any with organised crime. It was even suggested that what happened on the houseboat was murder, not suicide. In death, as in life, Cunanan remained an enigma.

Defending the authorities against charges of over-reacting and failing to take Cunanan alive, an FBI spokesman said: "With someone who is using desperate means and exhibiting this kind of violent behaviour, you have to be prepared for a very violent conclusion."

The investigators then looked even more closely at the owner of the houseboat in which Cunanan died. Forty-eight-year-old Torsten Reineck, a flamboyant homosexual, was the German manager of a gay health spa in Las Vegas. In 1992 he fled Germany, where he was wanted by the police, who had an international warrant out for him in connection with a $70,000 fraud in Leipzig. And like Versace he was also being investigated for possible tax evasion.

So had the two men been engaged in money laundering for the Mob? Was there a personal connection between the German, Versace and Cunanan? These were some of the questions for which the police and the press were seeking answers.

There were no signs of forced entry to the houseboat, which suggested that Cunanan might have had a key. Police searching the boat said they found a metal safety deposit box containing evidence linking Cunanan to the earlier murders, along with that of Versace. There was also a hit-list which Cunanan had drawn up – a list of prominent people he wanted to kill, Sylvester Stallone among them.

The police also found a TV set tuned to the local news station, and there was speculation that Cunanan had gleefully watched the manhunt. He had finally achieved what he had always wanted: to become the centre of the nation's attention. Psychologists believe that at this time he must have been in a state of euphoria.

The Versace family were full of praise for the way the murder was cleared up, but others felt that Cunanan's death had brought the investigation to a suspiciously neat conclusion. The Roman designer Gai Mattiolo said he thought it "pretty odd that within a week there can be the certainty of having solved the Versace case."

The FBI and the Miami police made no mention of the fact that for two months the serial killer was hiding under their noses. Now Nicole Ramitez-Murray, a former friend of Cunanan, lambasted the FBI: "They handled this case like the Keystone Cops. I think they bungled it right from the start. I don't think they took it seriously until there was a label, until there was an international name."

When the police did discover Cunanan's earlier Miami whereabouts he was long gone – his room at the Normandy Plaza motel was even searched first by a local television crew who beat the police to it. When the police did examine the room they reported finding a razor, shaved body hair and a woman's corset, adding weight to speculation that Cunanan sometimes dressed as a woman.

When Cunanan vanished after Versace's murder police and detectives were naturally depressed. They thought he had fled, perhaps back to the Philippines. They never guessed he was right under their noses. Apparently the FBI did not tell the police that its agents believed the killer was still in the area.

Erik Greenman, who shared an apartment with Cunanan in San Diego for a year, revealed that his roommate had plotted to kidnap the actor Tom Cruise and sexually torture him. He would seek out Cruise lookalikes in gay bars, referring to his nightly trips as "Tom Cruising." Then he would take the lookalikes to a bath house or a hotel to torture them with whips and chains.

Greenman said: "Andrew was passionately in love with Tom Cruise and wanted him sexually. He was totally obsessed." He said that Cunanan would play one vile pornographic film endlessly, saying he longed to re-enact it with the movie star. The scene showed a young man strapped to a chair, being tortured with an electric cattle prod.

"More than once I came home to find Andrew watching this shocking torture scene," Greenman recalled. "He'd say, 'I want to tie up Cruise, use him and make him beg for more.' But he hated Cruise's wife Nicole. He told Greenman that he'd have to kill her so he could have Tom all to himself. He also said he would kill Tom if he couldn't have him sexually.

"Andrew's mind was warped beyond repair. He had pictures of Tom Cruise plastered all over his bedroom. He'd rent five Cruise videos and spend the whole evening stopping them frame by frame, studying the actor's every gesture. He told me: 'Tom ages like fine wine. He's the perfect boy.' The actor was everything Andrew wanted in a lover – including the boyish frame and incredible smile. He used to describe bizarre sexual fantasies about dressing Cruise in full leather bondage outfits and dominating and humiliating him. He was so nuts about the movie star that every time he went to the bathroom he would grab an article about Cruise from his shrine and read it there."

There was more trouble when the marina caretaker who found Versace's killer was told by the police: "You won't get the $40,000 reward." Fernando Carreira lost out because he did not specifically tell the cops that the prowler he discovered was Cunanan. Although the 71-year-old caretaker continued to keep watch on the fugitive until the police arrived, the reward was for "information leading to the apprehension of Cunanan" – and the wanted man couldn't be apprehended because he was dead.

Richard Barreto said: "It is not my understanding that the caretaker provided information specifically with the intent of telling us where Cunanan was." This outraged the media and caused an outcry on television news and chat shows across the nation. The presenter of CNN's *Burden of Proof* crime show said: "How can the FBI expect folks to co-operate and help them if when they come to claim the reward, people are told, 'Tough, you can't have it after all'?"

It was reported that at least six film companies were planning movies based on Versace's murder. By a twist of irony that Cunanan would have appreciated, the biggest of the Hollywood studio announced that it was short-listing Keanu Reeves to play the killer – not Tom Cruise, but near enough...

But the biggest irony of all came with Andrew Cunanan's post-mortem. When pathologists examined the man whose murder spree was triggered by being told he was HIV positive, they found no sign of that affliction at all. He had no immune deficiency, only a mental one. He was not immune from his own evil.

3

SAL MINEO
Final Curtain For a Supporting Player

As a film star Sal Mineo was accustomed to sudden death. He achieved fame in 1955 as Plato, the psychotic juvenile delinquent from a wealthy background who ended up gunned down by the police in the classic James Dean movie *Rebel Without a Cause*.

He created such an impression in that role that he became typecast as a handsome young thug, usually destined to come to a sticky end. Just stepping out on to the street became quite a problem for the star who was becoming known as "The Switchblade Kid" – he was for ever being mobbed by girls.

Years passed, he made a lot of money, and then he died a different death. He simply went out of fashion. "You're not a hot property any more," his agents told him.

"And they were right," he later reflected. "I wasn't getting too many offers."

Then the time was to come when he would make headlines again...but not the kind anyone would have chosen for themselves.

If any actor came up the hard way and then peaked too soon, it was Sal Mineo. The son of Sicilian immigrants, he was born in New York's Harlem district in 1939. His father made coffins, and Sal grew up in the Bronx, to where his family moved and where of necessity he had to learn to take care of himself. He was no stranger to juvenile crime

– experience which was to help him identify with the characters he later portrayed.

Expelled from school at eight, he was a problem child. A series of special schools followed, where from time to time he was dragooned into taking part in plays, and found that he quite enjoyed acting.

Others enjoyed watching him on stage, and it was in a school play that he was spotted by a casting director. Sal Mineo was consequently whisked off to fill a small role opposite Eli Wallach in a stage production of Tennessee Williams's *The Rose Tattoo*.

More parts followed, and he made his Broadway debut in 1952 as a young prince in *The King and I* with Yul Brynner. After a two-year run in that show he moved on to Hollywood to play in films starring Charlton Heston and Tony Curtis.

His performance in *Rebel Without a Cause* brought him an Oscar nomination, followed by roles in *Giant, Exodus* and *The Longest Day*.

He was becoming seriously rich at a time when he lacked the maturity to handle his wealth.

"I made millions," he was to recall, "but I spent it freely. I spent it, and I don't regret it. I enjoyed those years from the time I started making money until I lost it. I had expensive cars, I had a big home in Beverly Hills, I put my sister and two brothers through college.

"I gave fabulous parties to which I invited fabulous people ... I was happy. A lot of people I know who have a lot of money don't know how to spend it. They don't know how to achieve happiness. I was living the way I wanted. And then I ceased being a hot property.

"There was this whole new craze, 'Let's get new faces.' And all of a sudden all the good roles I wanted went to the new faces... When I saw that I wasn't getting offered good roles, I knew things weren't going to get any better."

And they didn't. On a downward spiral, he did his best to adjust and diversify.

If he could no longer be a star actor, he decided, he

would have a shot at becoming a star director.

It was a gamble. Literally. He needed a thousand dollars to buy an option on a play he wanted to direct, and to get the money he went to Las Vegas.

There he played roulette each weekend for up to 12 hours a day. But he limited his gambling to Saturdays and Sundays by buying return tickets, which meant that he had to fly back to Los Angeles when each two-day period was up, whether he was winning or losing. Like this, he figured, he was exercising some self-discipline.

He won the money he needed, he directed the play and it was a big success. But it failed to bring him offers to direct other productions.

By now as an actor he was reduced to donning a mask to play a chimpanzee in the film *Escape from the Planet of the Apes*. Lean times continued. He sold his Hollywood house, rented a small flat near the notorious Sunset Strip in West Hollywood, and survived by directing more plays.

On February 12th, 1976, he was busy rehearsing *PS Your Cat is Dead*, a drama that was to open in Los Angeles in the following week. He was now 37, and his film career had virtually petered out, but he had high hopes of the new play. He drove home that night pleased with the rehearsals, and unaware that he was about to play a leading role in a real-life drama. It had no script and no title, but *Curtains for Sal Mineo* would do.

Having parked his blue Chevelle behind his apartment block, he began making his way down the dark alley to the entrance to the building. His scream was the other tenants' first intimation that something was wrong. Then they heard him cry, "My God, my God, help me!" This was followed by another scream, and then all was ominously quiet.

As his neighbours rushed out they glimpsed a fleeing man with long hair – some said it was fair, others described it as brown. Sal Mineo was lying on his back in the alley, stabbed in the heart, and with blood gushing from the wound in his chest.

One of the tenants tried mouth-to-mouth resuscitation. "He kept gasping," the neighbour said later. "After about five minutes his last breath went into me. That was the end of it."

It was also the beginning of endless speculation. Sal Mineo had not been robbed, so what was the killer's motive? Mineo was known to be hard up, so had he turned to drug-pushing to solve his financial problems? Had he been killed by a supplier to whom he owed money?

That line of investigation got nowhere, but another possibility seemed more promising. Mineo had been involved in helping to rehabilitate ex-convicts, so had one of those he befriended turned on him and killed him?

The actor was also rumoured to have been a bisexual sado-masochist, so was he killed by a disgruntled partner? That line of inquiry was reinforced when detectives examined his flat. Pin-ups of naked men decorated the walls. One photograph portrayed one of Mineo's friends wearing women's underwear. There was a pile of magazines featuring nude men and the books on the shelves were mostly of a homosexual nature. These discoveries strengthened the suspicion that the killer was a jilted lover.

More than coincidentally, the first play Mineo directed had a homosexual theme, and he was to have played a homosexual in *PS Your Cat is Dead*.

But the situation was confused by the knowledge that Mineo hadn't always been gay. "My hobby is girls," he boasted at the time when a newspaper labelled him "the teenagers' dreamboat."

He was once engaged to actress Jill Haworth, and when it was broken off they remained good friends, Mineo explaining, "I love Jill. I always will, but I'm not for marriage and kids. I've been on my own since I was about fifteen ... I need companionship, I need love and all the things that go with it, but I don't need the responsibility of married life. I like my freedom too much."

The police checked out his male friends. "GAYS FACE QUIZ OVER MINEO'S MURDER," said one headline.

But again the detectives drew a blank. None of Mineo's men friends became a suspect. They tried to raise $10,000 reward for information leading to the killer's arrest, but contributions added up to no more than a few hundred dollars.

As one friend remarked, "In this racket when you're not hot any more, or when you're cold, you're dead anyway. So a lot of people just shrugged, and turned the page on Sal's murder."

His obituaries played him as a born-to-lose character. His friend Peter Bogdanovich wrote in *Esquire*: "That Sal was stabbed to death in an alley was so horribly in keeping with so many of the movie deaths he died that its bitter irony might have amused him. After all, he had a black sense of humour..."

Another obituarist reported Mineo's death as an ironic escape from typecasting: "This time there were no searchlights hailing the American teenager gone berserk – only one man cutting up another ..."

Nearly two years passed, and it seemed that the case would remain unsolved. Then the wife of a man in a Michigan jail came forward to say her husband was Sal Mineo's killer. Theresa Williams claimed that her 21-year-old husband Lionel returned to their Los Angeles home on the night of the murder covered with blood.

"I just killed this dude in Hollywood," he told her, saying that he killed Sal Mineo with a hunting knife.

The former pizza deliveryman was now serving time in Michigan for forging a cheque and it transpired that he had bragged to a warder that he was Mineo's murderer. He was also overheard saying to another prisoner: "Have you ever killed anyone? It's very easy."

The man presumed by witnesses to have been Mineo's killer had left the scene in a small yellow car. Williams, the police learned, was driving a yellow Dodge Colt on that night. A hunting knife was tattooed on his arm – "almost as if he put the mark of Cain on himself," remarked a prosecutor.

Williams's record showed that he was suspected of committing a series of vicious muggings. Shortly after the murder he was arrested for robbery, and in a bid for leniency he offered information on Mineo's killing, claiming the actor was murdered in an argument about dope. But as Sal Mineo had no known drugs background, Williams's story was dismissed.

Now the case against the Michigan prisoner looked promising, but there was a problem. The long-haired man observed running from the crime scene was described by witnesses as white. Lionel Williams was black, his hair was short, and he denied everything.

From their files the police turned up an old photograph of the suspect. It portrayed a man with long brown hair – at that time, it transpired, Williams had his hair put through a straightening process, and wore it shoulder length. The witnesses assumed that the fleeing man was white because his hair was long and brown.

The police were confident that they had the right man, but the confusion over the suspect's colour was a weak link in their case. They needed more evidence, and the clincher was supplied by the Los Angeles County Forensic Science Center. Preserved there in formalin was a section of Sal Mineo's chest, incorporating the stab wound and the surrounding tissue.

At the time of the murder the Los Angeles coroner's office bought a selection of knives to assist research into stab wounds, which were becoming prevalent in the city. The coroner later recalled: "When the police arrived at our office they had a description obtained from Williams's wife of a hunting knife owned by her husband. She even knew its price – $5. 28. We had an exactly similar knife in our collection.

"Normally we don't insert a matching knife into a wound during a post-mortem because it would distort the incision. But now, because the tissues were fixed in formalin for storage, we could do so without such distortion. We inserted the blade of this knife in the wound and it fitted perfectly."

That was all the police needed. On January 5th, 1978, just four days before he was due to be released from prison, Lionel Williams was charged with Sal Mineo's murder.

"This man is a predator," prosecutor Michael Genelin told the court at Williams's trial in January, 1979. "He enjoyed brutalising people. These were not just street robberies but one incident after another where he inflicted pain and enjoyed it."

Found guilty, Williams was sentenced to serve 51 years to life. Why it took his wife so long to shop him was never disclosed. She certainly chose a very effective way of not having him back.

4

JOHN LENNON
Death At The Dakota

Two forces fought to control the mind of Mark David Chapman. Good against evil. Saint versus sinner.

Just before 11 p.m. on the chilly night of December 8th, 1980, the conflict was resolved in favour of the sinner. That was the moment when Chapman shot dead his idol, superstar John Lennon, in the shadows outside the former Beatle's luxury Manhattan home Chapman later told a clergyman: "I've been going through a torment – a struggle between good and evil, between right and wrong. I just gave in."

As Lennon lay dying in the arms of his screaming, hysterical wife Yoko Ono, Chapman calmly opened his treasured, dog-eared copy of J. D. Salinger's celebrated novel *The Catcher in the Rye*, sat down on a wall a few paces from where he had shot the superstar, and began to read. After his arrest he read the book in his cell and took it with him on every remand court appearance.

Six hours before he was killed, Lennon and his wife left their luxury apartment block, the Dakota, to go to a recording session. On the pavement was the usual knot of fans standing around hoping to get a glimpse of their idol or even his autograph. Among those who pushed forward was Mark Chapman, a dishevelled, 25-year-old, five feet eleven inches tall, out-of-work security guard. He was carrying 14 Beatle tape recordings in a satchel and the Beatle LP *Double Fantasy* in his hand.

He extended the LP to Lennon who, as he had done on thousands of other occasions, signed the sleeve, "John Lennon, 1980." The ex-Beatle then climbed into a waiting limousine with Yoko.

Chapman turned to a photographer in the crowd. "John Lennon signed my album," he gasped. "No one is going to believe me."

After the Lennons had gone, Chapman hung around for about two hours with a tall blonde girl aged about 20. The photographer, who had been keeping them company, then said he intended to leave, but Chapman told him: "I'd wait if I was you. You never know if you'll see him again." The photographer replied: "What do you mean? I always see him."

The photographer left, and so too did Chapman. Later Chapman, dressed in a leather jacket against the December cold, returned to the pavement outside the Dakota. Just before 11 p.m. he heard the car bringing the Lennons home from their engagement pull up outside.

He fell back into the shadows and as the couple emerged from their car stepped forward, calling, "Mr. Lennon?"

The ex-Beatle turned slowly, and saw the man who was about to kill him. Lennon had no chance to speak as Chapman dropped to his knees in the classic combat position, arms outstretched, both hands on the butt of a .38. From point-blank range he fired and fired again. Four shots ripped into his victim's body.

Lennon managed to stagger up six steps to a small office. His murderer watched with a smirk on his face.

"I'm shot," moaned Lennon, and fell down. For a moment, a dozen eye-witnesses stood in shocked silence. Then Yoko's scream rang out across the courtyard.

She rushed to her fallen husband and cradled him in her arms and began to cry. Then she appealed: "Help me, oh please help me."

Chapman dropped the gun. The Dakota's doorman ran up and kicked it away. Chapman paid no attention. Already a police car siren was beginning to sound in the distance.

"Do you know what you just did?" the doorman blurted out.

"I just shot John Lennon," Chapman replied.

The multi-millionaire former Beatle was wearing blue jeans and a red shirt. His chest was wet with blood.

Patrolmen Tony Palma and Herb Frauenberger, the first policemen to arrive, hauled Lennon into the back of their car. On the way to hospital Palma asked, "Are you John Lennon?" Convulsed with pain, Lennon's only response was a single moan.

Another patrol car took a sobbing, shaking Yoko to the hospital. She cried out, "Tell me it's not true. Tell me it's going to be all right."

Lennon was rushed to the emergency room in Manhattan's Roosevelt Hospital. Half a dozen specialists worked on him. Tubes and blood drips were everywhere. But it was hopeless. Within seconds he was dead from the multiple wounds to his chest.

Chapman was arrested without any difficulty and according to a police officer appeared "cool, calm and rational." There were massive police precautions as the bespectacled assassin arrived for a brief hearing at a hastily convened court. He was still wearing the blue serge trousers and fawn sweater he had on when he was arrested.

Judge Martin Rettinger, fearing a revenge bid from one of Lennon's grief-stricken fans, had a metal-screening device placed at the court door to detect any concealed weapons. Chapman did not speak during the short hearing.

The court was given a brief outline of his short career by his defence lawyer, Herbert Adlerberg. Chapman had been a mental institution patient and had twice tried to kill himself, the court was told. Almost certainly he would try to commit suicide again. His defence lawyer said he believed his client was incapable of understanding what he had done.

There were 12 outstanding warrants for his arrest,

dating back to 1972. They were for offences including armed robbery, burglary, abduction and possessing drugs.

Chapman was remanded until January 6th, 1981, and was sent to a criminal psychiatric ward in New York's Belle Vue Hospital. After the hearing his lawyer said his client "had a great admiration for Lennon." He had found Chapman "coherent in some respects, but confused about other areas."

As Chapman was being dubbed "the most hated man in America," a stunned generation of Beatles fans went into mourning for their murdered idol.

It emerged that the last words whispered by the star who gave the world the famous song *She Loves You, Yeah, Yeah, Yeah*, as he lay dying were, "Help me."

Lennon, who was 40, left behind him a wealth of music and the huge fortune he made from it. His talent and his money made him arrogant and unpredictable. The role he liked to play was the hard man, the irreverent rebel, the surly Scouse with a quickfire quip for every occasion.

Many who knew him said he was a soft man at heart. They thought of him as the original flower child, preaching a gospel of love and understanding, with key statements in his simple philosophy, like "All you need is love," and "Give peace a chance." He became the guru of a generation sickened by the Vietnam war and horrified by the prospect of an ever more violent and unfeeling future.

Others, like some of the scores of pressmen assigned to follow the escapades of the Beatles during the 1960s as they climbed upwards to their dizzy fame, felt that it wasn't all quite the rosy-tinted way the fans thought it was. But they had to keep quiet, for any criticism of the Beatles in that decade was regarded as heresy.

The upwards climb was so steep that it caused Lennon to proclaim tastelessly: "We're more popular than Jesus now. I don't know which will go first – rock'n' roll or Christianity." He later made a public apology for the remark.

Nor did all the Lennon philosophy bear deep scrutiny. In

the month that he was killed he said in a radio interview: "We're going to live or we're going to die. If we're dead we're going to have to deal with that; if we're alive we're going to have to deal with being alive. So worrying about whether Wall Street or the Apocalypse is going to come in the form of the great beast is not going to do us any good today."

Millions of fans drank in this sort of stuff, believing they were listening to words of great wisdom. Others understandably wondered what it was supposed to mean.

This was a problem with more than one set of rock 'n'roll exponents. They began to think that anything they did or said was above and beyond all criticism, even if it was trite.

But there was no disputing the Beatles' phenomenal success in the world of pop music. In their brief eight-year reign over the charts they transformed modern music. Their fame spilled out from Liverpool right across the world. They took America by a storm in a way that no British group has achieved before or since. In this extraordinary story John Lennon was the chief mover – the arch-Beatle.

Paul McCartney wrote many of the pretty tunes, George Harrison was the most gifted instrumentalist, Ringo Starr had mawkish charm. But it was Lennon who provided the Beatles' unique bitter-sweet quality: the haunting irony and sad humour, the questioning and protest that lay beyond the jingles.

Lennon, the creator, was also probably the main agent in the break-up of the group. Once that happened, buttressed by his vast accumulated wealth, he seemed to become more and more a confused figure, always seeking a new and different role.

During the life of the group he was by far the most outrageous of the Beatles – themselves the most outrageous group of entertainers ever to take the world by storm. He also became the leader of the Swinging Sixties crusade against society's taboos about sex and drugs.

In the early years Lennon was outgoing and outspoken, an expansive extrovert who was often irritating. But for the last five years of his life, after the Beatles' break-up, he became the Howard Hughes of the rock world, locking himself away with his wife and their son Sean and living the life of a hermit in the centre of Manhattan.

The man who had £100 million and earned £5 million a year in royalties became a "house-husband" – devoting his life to baking the daily bread and raising his son.

It was a far cry from the hard life he lived as a youth in Liverpool. Lennon, born October 9th, 1940, was the son of a porter who deserted his family three years later. The father turned up on Lennon's doorstep after his son became a star – and had the door slammed in his face.

Lennon's mother Julia died in a car crash when John was 14. But even before her death he had chosen to live with his favourite aunt, Mrs. Mary Smith, whom he called Aunt Mimi. While still a teenager, he went to Liverpool College of Art, where he met Cynthia Powell, the girl who later became his first wife.

There too he teamed up with some friends to make music – Paul McCartney and later George Harrison. Ringo Starr joined the group much later.

The embryonic Beatles got themselves up and running as a result of three big breaks. First they were booked as a £7-a-night act in Liverpool's Cavern Club, where they built up an enthusiastic following of local fans. Then they were booked to play at the Star Club in Hamburg, where they developed an energetic stage act which sent the audience wild. After that, local record store owner Brian Epstein, a shrewd, hard-headed businessman, heard them and became their manager.

Their first single, "*Love Me Do*," sold 100,000 copies and entered the charts towards the end of 1962. The following year "*Please, Please Me*," became the first of 22 million-selling singles, heralding the arrival of Beatlemania.

Thereafter, young girls screamed and fainted at Beatles' concerts and young men sported Beatle hair-cuts – daring over-the-ear styles. And they wore "Beatle suits" shorn of their lapels.

Behind the scenes, though, it wasn't all squeaky clean. During a four-year spell Lennon's mind was nearly blown by drugs. He said: "I went on LSD and I must have had a thousand trips." At 17 he started on pep pills, and then regularly smoked cannabis and experimented with heroin and cocaine.

His only other "escape" was to come under the powerful influence of the Beatles' guru Marharishi Yogi.

Lennon's passion for LSD was celebrated in one of the Beatles' hits, "*Lucy in the Sky with Diamonds.*" Mums and Dads thought it was just a pleasant song. But the teenagers caught on to the song's main initials of LSD.

Lennon claimed he even smoked cannabis in the toilets at Buckingham Palace when the Beatles were waiting to collect their MBE medals from the Queen in 1965. Two years after that he was fined £150 after a police raid on his home revealed supplies of cannabis. He was back on drugs in the 1970s and told of being "stoned for a month or two." He added: "God, it was terrifying."

The strain of being the Beatles began to show in the late Sixties when the group was producing some of its best music. The final split came in 1969.

Lennon married Yoko Ono that year and dropped out of the limelight. In 1980 he released his first record for years and fans hoped a Beatles reunion would be on the cards. That dream was dashed for ever by the crazed gunman Mark Chapman, wielding his .38 from the pavement outside the Lennon home.

What was the demon that drove Chapman to kill? He was born in Fort Worth, Texas, in May, 1955, and grew up in America's Deep South in the small town of Decatur, Georgia, during the Beatle-dominated Sixties of hard rock, hard drugs, easy sex and youthful protest. He was only 13 when he became involved in the drug scene, tripping on LSD, pot, mescaline and heroin. Like most of his generation, he became an ardent Beatles fan, and a great admirer of John Lennon.

Then at 16 he surprisingly kicked the drug habit by himself. The reason was that the Southern boy had rediscovered God at a fiery evangelical rally. Included in this revelation, apparently, was an apostasy turning him against rock-'n'-roll – fellow students were astonished to discover Chapman suddenly arguing against the "perverse" influence of rock music. Among his prime targets were his former idols the Beatles and Lennon in particular.

Leaving college, Chapman became a YMCA co-ordinator working for refugees. At the same time he fell in love with a deeply devout Southern girl, Jessica Blankinship. The rot set in again, though, after he flunked studies to qualify him as a full-time YMCA co-ordinator or missionary. He also lost Jessica, and soon after that his parents divorced.

"My life has gone," he sobbed to friends. It was a sharp contrast to the quietly confident youngster who told school friends in December, 1975: "About five years from now one of us will do something famous."

Eventually he fled despondently to Honolulu, Hawaii, in search of an escape through suicide. Twice he tried to kill himself by stringing a hose from the exhaust pipe into his car and sealing himself in. But on both occasions a passer-by broke in and rescued him.

"I was such a failure, I even failed at killing myself," Chapman told his friend and former YMCA mentor David Moore.

In Hawaii he met and married another deeply Christian girl, a Japanese-American named Gloria Abe. The similarities with the personal life of John Lennon were becoming chillingly obvious. He had taken shooting lessons, become a crack shot, and found himself a job as a security guard at a luxury Honolulu apartment building.

About this time his bizarre obsession with Lennon was rekindling itself inside his twisted mind. On October 10th, 1980, two months before he shot the superstar, he quit his job and signed himself out as "John Lennon." In the two months between then and the murder, friends noticed a marked deterioration in his mental condition.

On June 22nd, 1981, Chapman avoided a full-blown trial by pleading guilty to murdering the superstar. His plea was accepted by Judge Dennis Edwards sitting in the Manhattan Supreme Court, despite his own lawyer's claim that Chapman was too crazy to make up his own mind.

Chapman spent an hour in secret session persuading the judge he was sane enough to decide for himself. The judge later said he had taken the extremely rare step of allowing Chapman to plead behind closed doors because he wanted to be absolutely certain that the accused man understood what he was doing. He would pass sentence on August 24th after one final re-examination by psychiatrists.

Chapman, in a bullet-proof vest because of fears of an assassination attempt, said nothing in court. His lawyer, Jonathan Marks, said that his client changed his original plea of not guilty by virtue of temporary insanity after hearing "messages from God" on June 8th and June 10th.

Mr. Marks said: "When God came into it, my advice went out of the window. It's been virtually impossible for me to have any meaningful dialogue with my client since then. It is impossible to bend him."

Mr. Marks talked after hearing about his client's bizarre interest in J. D. Salinger's novel *The Catcher in the Rye*. The book, which was cult reading in the Fifties, tells the story of an archetypal mixed-up teenager named Holden Caulfield, who has to undergo psychiatric treatment. The hero is revealed as a sensitive young man disturbed by growing up in a world full of adult 'phoneys.' Mr. Marks said: "The reason why Chapman shot John Lennon was because he wanted to promote the book and get everyone in the world reading it. He saw that as the bizarre special mission he had been assigned to.

"But the so-called messages from God have changed all that. My personal belief is that Mark Chapman is insane.

And I believe that if the case had gone to trial we would have proved that."

However, the lawyer accepted one fear that Chapman confided to the judge in secret. He had serious doubts whether he was sufficiently stable to withstand a long trial without suffering a nervous breakdown.

In court, Chapman, who was smuggled in and out in a tight security operation, showed no sign of regretting his crime. But later lawyer Marks said: "Since that 'God message' he has for the first time expressed to me during my visit to him in jail feelings of remorse and sorrow for Lennon's family. He was also deeply worried about threats that could endanger witnesses and members of the jury if there had been a full trial."

Chapman's change of heart also spared Lennon's widow the ordeal of having to relive from the witness box the night he was gunned down. Yoko was not in court for the final hearing involving Chapman.

During the month he was in custody before being sentenced Chapman was held in isolation in New York's tough Rikers Island Prison. Other prisoners threatened to kill him and prison officers had to keep a suicide watch. According to lawyer Marks, "Suicide is a very real worry." Some psychiatrists even insisted that because of the killer's previous suicide attempts, the assassination was just another confused bid to kill himself.

When Chapman was finally brought before the court for sentencing in August, 1981, prosecutor Allen Sullivan said: "He killed Lennon because he was available and because he was easy. He was interested only in what his little finger would do to bring him attention."

Dr. Daniel Schwartz said Chapman was a schizophrenic with a narcissistic personality. As a boy of ten he had difficulty in socialising and relating to his elders. Instead he engaged in an imaginary world of little people. Chapman had told the doctor: "I have control over their lives. They treat me like a king."

As Chapman grew older, said the doctor, he believed his

mind was a computer. Red, green and yellow lights flashed to help him come to decisions.

In August, 1979, he was battling for his sanity. The computer had been taken over by an imaginary government and various committees now dictated his actions. Throughout this turmoil, however, his idol remained steadfastly John Lennon. He tried to model himself on the superstar, and the closer he identified with Lennon the more he believed he was Lennon.

"In the end he considered he was the real Lennon and that John Lennon was a fake," said Dr. Schwartz.

While in custody Chapman claimed that devils had forced him to kill Lennon. His behaviour in prison was often wild and irrational. He tried to tear out his hair, and when that failed he cut it short. He threatened to kill prison officers and in one outburst smashed a TV set and a radio. He went on hunger strike until told he would be fed intravenously if his life was in danger.

Prosecutor Allen Sullivan told the court that Chapman's conversations with the judge "amply demonstrated that he had knowingly, intentionally and of his own free will" taken the decision to ditch his "non-responsibility plea."

When the submissions were finished Chapman was asked if he had anything to say before sentence was passed. He stood up in the hushed courtroom and said: "I am going to read you a passage from *The Catcher in the Rye*." He opened his copy of the novel and read out: "I have to catch everybody every day. That is all I do every day. I just be the Catcher in the Rye."

When he sat down again Judge Edwards read out the sentence which, he said, had to be seen as a deterrent to others. Chapman was jailed for 20 years to life.

Singing stars reacting to the news of their idol's murder were effusive in their praise for Lennon's generosity in helping other show business people. Cilla Black, whose singing career was launched by Lennon, wept when she was told.

"My first reaction was that it was a very sick joke," she

said. "I felt so upset that I immediately had to get away from people and went to my room. Why would anyone want to kill him? I just can't think.

"But I could never understand why John should want to live in such a violent place as New York. I wouldn't bring up a cat there."

Lennon spotted Cilla's talent when he heard her singing at Liverpool's Cavern Club in the early sixties. The Beatles were then at the beginning of their own fabulous career.

"John told their manager, Brian Epstein, about me," said Cilla. "At first, Brian wasn't too keen, but John told him to give me a chance. I owe everything to John. He committed himself 100 per cent to the music business."

Mick Jagger of the Rolling Stones was "shattered." He was given the news in Paris, where he was recording a new album, and said: "I knew and liked John for 18 years. But I don't want to make a casual remark now at such an awful moment for his family, millions of fans and friends."

Cliff Richard said: "John Lennon was one of the very few people who could really be called rock-and-roll greats. We shall miss him for a long time." Billy J. Kramer, another Swinging Sixties pop star who owed his career to Lennon, said: "He gave me my first hit record, '*Do You Want To Know a Secret?*' John recorded it on tape and then played it to Brian Epstein, with instructions to let me make a disc of it. It was a terrific song and went straight to No. 1 in 1963. That was how incredibly generous John was."

Lennon later provided Billy with another chart-topper, called "*Bad for Me*."

Paul McCartney said: "John was a great man. His death is a bitter, cruel blow – I really loved the guy. He was one of the best. He will be sadly missed by the whole world. I can't tell you how much it hurts to lose him."

Lennon's first wife Cynthia was told the news while staying with ex-Beatle Ringo Starr's former wife, Maureen, in Surrey. Choking back tears she said: "We're all terribly upset. Julian has remained close to his father over the past few years and was hoping to follow a career in music."

Even US President Jimmy Carter joined in the tributes to the former Beatle who made America his home. In his last month of office – he was about to stand down in favour of President-elect Ronald Reagan – the outgoing President said: "John Lennon helped create the music and the mood of our time. His spirit, the spirit of the Beatles – brash and earnest, ironic and idealistic all at once – became the spirit of the whole generation. His work as an artist and musician was far from done.

"In the songs he compiled, both in partnership with Paul McCartney and in his own right, he leaves an extraordinary and permanent legacy."

For President-elect Reagan the shooting was "a great tragedy." The killing showed that America had to stamp out violence on the streets.

That was a comment that turned out to be bitterly ironic. For three months later a gunman tried to kill the President just after he had made another speech deploring crime on the streets of America. He was wounded, taken to hospital and released after a few days.

5

VICKI MORGAN
Sex and the Superstore Boss

To anyone who might have been listening, it must have sounded like a story as old as the hills. She was still in her teens, killing time in a coffee shop between appointments made in the hope of becoming a model. He was 54, more than old enough to be her father. And he was overtly chatting her up.

As they drank their cappuccini while he gave her the talk at an outdoor table on Hollywood's Sunset Strip, he offered to find her all the work she needed as a model and an actress. He had connections, he told her confidently.

And Vicki Morgan, young as she was, sensed that he did have connections. He talked like a big shot, but he looked like one too. Her intuition was dead right. He was Alfred Bloomingdale, heir to the department store that bore his name, and founder of the Diner's Club.

She gave him her phone number without expecting to hear from him again. But she did. They were to mean a lot to each other.

Vicki's life had not been easy. Her father had deserted the family in her infancy, leaving her mother to bring up three children on welfare pay-outs. Four years later Vicki's mother remarried, and the family settled in Montclair, California. But Vicki's stepfather died when she was 13, and four years later she had a child by a high-school sweetheart.

At 18 she realised that if she was going to make anything of her life she would have to get where the action was – and it wasn't in Montclair. She knew she was beautiful, and she was determined to make the most of it, because it was the only asset she had. Leaving her son with her mother, she set off for Hollywood.

Within a few days Alfred Bloomingdale phoned, just as he had promised. He had set up an appointment for her, he told her, with a well-known film producer. All that came of that was a chance meeting with Cary Grant, followed by a brief affair with him.

The producer thought that Vicki was too young and inexperienced for him to be able to help her. But Cary Grant thought she was more than qualified to share his bed.

So did Alfred Bloomingdale. Within weeks of splitting with Grant, Vicki Morgan became the middle-aged playboy's mistress. But there was more to this than just sleeping with him, as she soon discovered. Bloomingdale was a sado-masochist. In order to climax he had to beat and be beaten.

A woman friend of Bloomingdale warned her in advance: "Alfred has a real interest in you and I'm here to tell you that he is going to beat you up...he does that to all the hookers he sees. He'll probably tie you up. He wants me to let you know that you are special to him, and he'll make some special allowances for you."

Vicki's first sexual encounter with the wealthy store-owner lived up to all that her confidante had forecast. After what she called "Alfred's Marquis de Sade bit" was over, she was shown the "special allowances." These took the form of monthly cheques ranging from $10,000 to $18,000. In his own way, Bloomingdale had a genuine affection for the naive girl from Montclair, and she in turn became fascinated by him and his worldliness.

Despite the nature of that first sexual encounter, $10,000 to $18,000 a month was enough to make a girl with few other prospects think twice before walking out on this generous provider. Bloomingdale called in two prostitutes to beat both himself and each other. Only after this stimulation could he rise to the occasion: his first coupling with Vicki, who also received a good thrashing. She also discovered that each session with Alfred would be rounded off with a bare-bottom spanking.

Several times a week she would watch Bloomingdale strip before he beat her. He would use silk ties to bind the wrists of other women present before he lashed their buttocks with a belt. Then he would get them to go down on their hands and knees, straddling them as he rode around the room drooling on to their backs. But it was only with Vicki that he would have intercourse.

"Wasn't that fun?" he would ask at the end of each orgy, and Vicki knew better than to say "No." The allowance he paid her came in the form of cheques from companies he controlled. Her part of the deal was to provide constant companionship and what Alfred called "therapy."

For Vicki part of his attraction was his influence in high places. A member of what was called Ronald Reagan's "kitchen cabinet," her elderly lover was tipped to become an ambassador. After Reagan became president, Bloomingdale was to become a member of the Foreign Intelligence Advisory Board, which was responsible for CIA undercover operations. Meanwhile he found Vicki another job. In the 1980 presidential campaign she was appointed George Bush's driver and guide.

Moving in such circles, she became privy to a lot of secrets. She was later to tell her lawyer, Marvin Mitchelson, that some of the things she knew made the Watergate scandal seem tame in comparison.

Through her association with Bloomingdale she was also involved in shenanigans with the political élite. They enjoyed group oral sex and other erotic diversions at a Hollywood Hills house in which Bloomingdale had installed hidden video cameras in every room, the three toilets included.

Every taste was catered for. A personable young gay, Marvin Pancoast, was part of this scene, and he was to become Vicki's friend and a key player in the tragedy that was to follow. For Vicki was way out of her depth in a dangerous world which had ramifications she would never understand. The protection provided by the ageing Bloomingdale couldn't last for ever, and she already knew more than was good for her about his associates.

As a kind of life insurance, Bloomingdale gave Vicki the custody of the tapes of all those orgies. When he was no longer around, her mere possession of them should yield her a steady income from top people anxious that they should never be played. For those tapes were dynamite.

But instead of tucking them away safely in a bank-vault, Vicki stacked them on a shelf along with other tapes in the house Bloomingdale rented for her in Beverly Hills. It seems that in her naiveté she didn't realise the implications of what had been filmed.

Meanwhile her high life continued. Although Bloomingdale had a wife, that didn't stop him taking Vicki along as well when he toured the world. They would travel separately, but wherever Bloomingdale went – London, Paris, Rome – Vicki was never far away, on hand to satisfy her lover's violent desires.

A hiccup in their relationship came in 1974, however, when for a time Vicki took up with the later to be disgraced financier Bernie Kornfield. She also had an affair with the King of Morocco. Both were generous lovers, but it was Bloomingdale whose continuing financial support gave Vicki security, and it was to him that she eventually returned. By now, to those who didn't know the score, he was introducing her as his daughter.

During their estrangement period, Vicki had also had a brief marriage.

She was later to claim that when she went back to Bloomingdale she stipulated that she was no longer to be on the receiving end of his sadistic practices. As his "therapist" she was to monitor his excesses with other women, cautioning him when she thought he was going too far.

"I mean," she explained, "when he got too rough with other women in the private group sessions, I would give him 'the look' because I could see he was hurting – seriously hurting – someone. Then he would calm down."

Vicki's close acquaintances also included Alexei Goodarzi, who presided over Washington's Rotunda Restaurant and was believed to be a double-agent, serving both the CIA and the Iranian secret police. His fate three years later was a pointer to the risky nature of the company Vicki was keeping. He was found behind the wheel of his new Porsche, his brains splattered over the dashboard by three bullets fired into the back of his head.

Living high on the vine in Hollywood usually has a hidden cost to it, and this was so with Vicki Morgan. In 1979 she booked herself into a short-stay mental hospital for treatment for depression.

Twelve years into her relationship with Bloomingdale, he learned that he had not long to live. He therefore took steps to ensure Vicki's future financial security. He arranged, in the event of his death, for her to be paid an ongoing allowance of $10,000 a month through com-panies he owned.

When he died of cancer at the age of 66 in August, 1982, however, it transpired that the arrangements he had made for Vicki were not as watertight as he supposed. Although he gave written instructions that her name should be "included in all contracts so that this cannot be taken away from her in the event of my incapacitation or absence," his widow blocked the allowance and a judge dismissed Vicki's $5 million palimony suit against the Bloomingdale estate.

"A thorough consideration of the material facts," ruled Judge Christian Markey, "leads inescapably to the conclusion that the relationship between Morgan and Bloomingdale was no more than that of a wealthy, older paramour and a young, well-paid mistress."

The relationship was "founded on meretricious sexual services" in which sex was for hire, an arrangement which was illegal in California. So on those grounds Vicki's bid for an income for life from the Bloomingdale estate was rejected.

Now 30, she was reduced to sharing a condominium in the San Fernando Valley's Studio City with her old friend Marvin Pancoast, and in the first week of July, 1983, they were about to be evicted for non-payment of the $1,000-a-month rent.

Vicki also had her son to support, and to make ends meet she had sold all her jewellery and her Mercedes convertible. She and Pancoast had been going halves with the rent, but even so it proved too much for them. Vicki still had those too-hot-to-handle tapes, but she failed to recognise them as a nest-egg, or to realise that they endangered her life.

Pancoast worked for a Hollywood talent-spotting agency, and she had first met him in 1979 when they were both patients in the same mental hospital. Pancoast's problem was a history of mental instability. Their friendship endured and Pancoast helped Vicki gather evidence for her palimony suit, as she couldn't afford to pay private investigators.

He also introduced her to an agent to represent her in negotiations concerning a book she proposed to produce in collaboration with a ghost-writer, Gordon Basichis. The book's projected title was *Alfred's Mistress*.

No one, apart from the late Alfred Bloomingdale, gave Vicki more support than the 33-year-old gay man now sharing her accommodation. So it was a more than troubled Marvin Pancoast who walked up to the desk sergeant at a Los Angeles police station on Thursday, July 7th, 1983, and announced that he had just bludgeoned Vicki Morgan to death with a baseball bat.

Strangely, Pancoast had not so much as a speck of blood on him, yet when Patrolman Kenneth Henckle went to the condominium he found blood spattered everywhere in the room where Vicki's corpse lay on a king-sized bed.

The officer had no trouble entering. The front door

wasn't locked, and the living-room was untidy with packing cases scattered about in readiness for Vicki's move. The door to the master bedroom was ajar, and Henckle stepped inside to see Vicki lying dead in a bloodstained yellow shirt and bikini panties.

There was blood on the walls, the ceiling and the floor, and a baseball bat lay across the body. Apparently without thought of any fingerprints that might be on the bat, Henckle moved it to one side in order to check Vicki's pulse for any sign of life. There was none, the patrolman reported, as he radioed the desk sergeant.

Detective William Welch arrived to find that the place appeared to have been turned over by someone looking for something. Although packing for the move had been in progress, that didn't explain the way the contents of drawers were strewn around.

Twenty or more video-cassettes were in a cabinet, each labelled with the name of a movie. The detective didn't list or scan them. He assumed they were what their labels said, and left them where they were.

He put the baseball bat into a plastic bag as evidence. Oddly, it wasn't bloodstained. And at Pancoast's subsequent trial for Vicki's murder the detective admitted that neither the bat nor the condominium were examined for fingerprints. Neither were pills on Vicki's bedside table analysed for their drug content.

Pancoast was said by his sister, giving evidence, to be all too susceptible to brain-washing. His lawyer, who had known him since he was 14, recalled that once Pancoast even confessed to murders committed by the Manson clan. Now he withdrew his admission that he killed Vicki, claiming that he must have been hypnotised while unconscious into believing he was the killer.

Basichis the ghost-writer was among those who testified at Pancoast's trial. He said that Pancoast came in late the night before the murder. He paced backwards and forwards and seemed on edge.

"That wasn't like him," Basichis told the court. "Then at

2 a.m. he was on the phone talking to someone. I stayed, made love to Vicki, and then we talked until 7.30 a.m. and recorded some more of her memoirs. Before I left she confided in me that she was afraid of being murdered. I have a feeling that someone with knowledge of the Bloomingdale tapes had approached her, possibly through Pancoast, with a proposal for blackmail."

According to the Los Angeles County coroner, Vicki was beaten to death the following night at around 2 a.m.

"I read Marvin's confession," Basichis said later. "He walks into a police station and voluntarily confesses. No one ever asks him, 'Was anyone with you in the apartment?' No one said, 'Should we go over this again?' It seems strange."

Stranger still was the fact that not only was there no blood on the suspect, there was none either on any of his other clothes found in the condominium.

"This is really a story of police negligence," said Anne Louise Bardach, joint author of a book about Vicki Morgan. "The scene of the crime was not sealed until twenty-four hours after the murder. What kind of police work is that? It's unheard of. People could just walk in and walk out, and they did. If there were any sex tapes in the condo, then they could easily have disappeared during those twenty-four hours."

Another mystery was how Pancoast got to the police station, which was four miles from the crime scene. He left his car parked outside the condominium, and he couldn't remember the journey. He could not have walked the distance in the time available, so did he take a taxi? No one knows, because the police did not bother to check.

It was known that on the night of the murder he left the condominium about midnight, returning shortly afterwards accompanied by Basichis and four other men. The group arrived in two cars, Basichis having come solely to collect his own vehicle, which he had earlier left parked outside Vicki's home.

The identities of the other men never became known, or

their whereabouts while Vicki was being bludgeoned to death.

It was not until four days after the murder that the police showed an interest in the tapes. Then Detective Welch suddenly displayed an urgent need for them. At least some of them had been taken to the home of Vicki's mother in Montclair, along with the victim's other possessions. Welch had them brought back and handed over to the district attorney.

This move was prompted by a revelation from another attorney. Robert Steinberg announced that two days after the murder three of the tapes were delivered to him by an anonymous blonde woman. He said they showed members of President Reagan's government "at play" – showed them in a way that could bring down the administration.

But when a court ordered Steinberg to surrender the tapes to the authorities he had another shock in store. He revealed that since his disclosure that they were in his possession they had been stolen from his office. It was suspected that they had been bought or otherwise procured by someone who had stashed them away safely to protect the Reagan administration.

Soon to be locked away conveniently too, was Marvin Pancoast. He had absolutely no motive for the murder and few believed him guilty. Many suggested he was simply the fall-guy, a pawn in a game with high stakes.

He pleaded not guilty and told his lawyer he had no recollection of attacking Vicki. She was alive and well and watching television with him when he nodded off. He awoke feeling sick and dizzy. He was conscious of a strange, powerful "medical" smell which suggested he had been chloroformed or otherwise rendered unconscious.

When he came round Vicki was lying dead on the bed. Although he heard water running in the bathroom – was the killer still there, cleaning up? – he was too confused to assess the situation. He just assumed that with Vicki dead and he alone with her, he must be somehow responsible.

He was still far from "with it" when he arrived at the police station. He didn't know how he got there, or why he made the rambling, disjointed statement which was to put him behind bars.

He had also, however, told a *Los Angeles Times* reporter that although he loved Vicki as a sister, "that didn't stop me from smashing her skull. I just wanted her to go to sleep and leave me alone that night. I wasn't angry, I was just tired. I'd been working with her, helping with the move."

At his trial, which began on June 12th, 1984, much was made of the testimony of Vicki's mother. She said that Pancoast called at her apartment on the night before her daughter's death. When he left he took the baseball bat belonging to Vicki's son, putting it in his car.

Pointing out that there was no proof that the bat was the murder weapon, defence attorney Charles Matthews said that Pancoast's confession was prompted by his masochistic urge to take the blame for someone else's crime. "There is no proof at all that Marvin Pancoast did anything at all, except to say that he killed Vicki Morgan," claimed Matthews, suggesting there was a cover-up by the authorities.

Pancoast's conflicting accounts served only to suggest that he knew little more than anyone else about what really happened on the night of the murder. After all, he had been confined in mental institutions on at least four occasions, and he was still receiving treatment at the time of the murder. The most significant evidence, it seemed, was neither Pancoast's confession nor his denial. It was the total absence of any blood on him.

But the jury didn't see it that way. They not only found him guilty, but they also decided he was sane at the time of the murder. On September 14th, 1984, he was sentenced to 25 years for the killing.

It was a verdict which doubtless satisfied those anxious to bring the affair to a quick close before it did any further damage to the Reagan administration.

For others, Vicki Morgan's description of Ronald Reagan's close friend Alfred Bloomingdale acquired a sad significance. "Alfred was the most fascinating man I ever met in my whole life," she said.

So he was. And he fascinated her to death.

6

FREDDIE MILLS
Fall-guy for the Racketeers

When British boxing was enjoying its golden age in the first two decades after the Second World War, names like Bruce Woodcock, Don Cockell, Freddie Mills, Jack London, Johnny Williams and a dozen or so others pulled sell-out crowds to the ringside. The reason for that was not just for their magnificent boxing skills, as for the kind of men they were – friendly, honest, disarming sportsmen for whom a fair fight was as important as winning.

They were the kind of men of whom post-war austerity Britain was rightfully proud, for they carried the flag of fair play to the four corners of the globe.

Given that he flourished in that era, given the kind of first-class, amiable sportsman that he was, the sudden, mysterious death of Freddie Mills left a cloud over the fight game that has never lifted. For Freddie, the world light-heavyweight champion for two glittering years, was one of boxing's great characters and in the 1960s arguably the most popular sportsman in Britain.

There was no arrogance, no side, none of the hubris, such as you meet regularly in today's so-called superstars about Freddie. In the ring he had the speed of a panther and the courage of a lion laced with skill and technique that was a delight to watch. But outside the ring he was just an ordinary unaffected man in the street, and that too was a delight to watch.

Freddie Mills was born on June 26th, 1919, in Bournemouth. His family were working class people; his father earned a living of sorts dealing in second-hand goods. Freddie left school at 14, having impressed no one academically – he had spelling problems all his life – and started work as a milk roundsman.

His interest in boxing was developed by a fellow-milk roundsman and two years after starting work he went in for a novices' boxing contest. He was entered in three fights, won all by a knock-out and took the prize for best boxer in the competition. At just 16 Freddie Mills was bustling forward on his way to world fame.

Before he was 17 he was signed as a professional and had a manager under contract named Bob Turner. He won eight of his first ten fights by knock-outs.

But in those pre-war days there wasn't much money in boxing and there were plenty of fighters around. To make some cash, Freddie became a fairground boxer, issuing open invitations to all comers. In 1940 he volunteered for the RAF, became an air force PT instructor, and met Ted Broadribb, the manager who was to take him to world-championship class.

Broadribb's daughter, Christine, was married to another boxer, South African heavyweight Don McCorkindale, but the marriage was already flat out on the canvas when Freddie appeared. The McCorkindales parted on the best of terms and Freddie Mills married Christine, thereby becoming his manager's son-in-law. The happy couple bought a house on Denmark Hill, in south London, and in due time Christine, who already had a son named Donnie by McCorkindale, produced two daughters.

For the next nine years Freddie Mills's career glittered, soaring upwards to the stars. On the way to world title fame he knocked out Jock McAvory in one round, then KO'd the great Len Harvey in two rounds to win the British and Empire light-heavyweight championship. He lost only to the American Gus Lesnevich, who was then world light-heavy champion, but came back to beat him for the world title in 1948.

For two years he remained the undisputed champion of the world. Then, in 1950, along came the American Joey Maxim to demolish him and end the British champ's sparkling career. After that defeat Freddie Mills decided to hang up his gloves. He had done well out of boxing, and certainly boxing had done well out of him. At 31 he could afford to retire.

Or could he?

Side by side with his boxing career, Freddie had developed a business career. He bought and sold property in the South London area for letting in a modest way, building up a portfolio which gave him sufficient income not to have to work when he hung up his gloves.

In 1946 he had also bought, with three partners, a Chinese restaurant in London's Charing Cross Road, on the fringe of Soho. Known as The Freddie Mills Chinese Restaurant it became a London landmark, the place to be seen eating. The business was profitable for around 17 years, during which time Freddie bought out two of the partners, leaving just himself and an actor named Andy Ho as the sole owners.

By 1962 there were a lot of Chinese restaurants in London and they were no longer smart places to eat. Freddie and Andy Ho took stock of their business and decided to make big changes. They closed it down, refurbished it as a night-club, and four months later, in May, 1963, the Freddie Mills Nite Spot opened in the revamped premises.

The re-vamp cost a lot of money by the standards of the time. It was said to be initially priced at £6,000, but as generally happens in building construction, the final figure was twice as much. It has been cited as a reason why Freddie Mills began to have money troubles, but the truth is that he could more than afford that sum, and from all accounts the club always made operating profits.

What happened next was one of the sadder reflections of

the "Swinging Sixties." For besides Chinese restaurants, the capital was also attracting protection racketeers. And one of their prime targets was any night-time business in and around Soho.

Indeed a "nite spot" in Soho at that time meant only one thing to the punters – a place where men could go, buy drinks, get girls, euphemistically called "hostesses," and get sex, albeit at an exorbitant price. A sort of legalised brothel, in fact.

At first, Freddie and Andy Ho had decided that there would be no girls, no hostesses in their nite spot. But a few months after the glitzy opening night celebrations by Freddie's big-name chums in show business, profits began to drop. The punters didn't want a club without girls, so they looked around to find clubs that provided what they wanted. They abandoned Freddie Mills's place and stayed away until Freddie and his partner had to agree that the customers had called the tune. Hostesses were hired immediately, and silk-stockinged legs were draped over bar stools until well into the small hours.

All Freddie Mills's friends agreed that this was definitely not the sort of thing that Mr. Nice Guy Freddie would dabble in. So why did he dabble in it? The answer, everyone said, was that he was incredibly naive. He probably knew that after re-opening in its new guise the business would have to have hostesses, but he hoped it wouldn't. When finally he had to hire them he knew the sort of things that might go on but genuinely thought that they would not go on in his club. Nothing is worse for a business than an owner who doesn't understand what is going on, and Freddie Mills, from most accounts, didn't understand what was going on in his business. And in his naiveté, it has been suggested, he sank deeper and deeper into the hands of the racketeers who fastened their greasy, greedy fingers on just this kind of "business."

It didn't take long for others to fasten on to Freddie's affairs, either. A national daily newspaper published a story that one of his employees was running a call-girl racket from the nite spot. Freddie actually went to see the editor protesting that the newspaper had got it all wrong. In the newspaper office the editor produced evidence indicating that they had got it all right, that some of his hostesses were prostitutes. Freddie Mills had to accept it then – but he left the office shaking his head in disbelief.

Reporters who were keeping an eye on Freddie's place noticed that among the regular customers were the Kray brothers, who had their own table at the centre of the club. The Krays were East End boxers, and as everyone knew, they commanded a lot of the rackets, including the extortion racket.

So we come to July 24th, 1965, a little more than two years after the Chinese restaurant had been turned into a nite spot.

Freddie Mills spent most of that Saturday cleaning his private swimming pool. He did a bit of shopping and some gardening, in the course of which he spoke to a number of different people all of whom would afterwards say he was in the best of spirits. He had an afternoon siesta and an early evening meal at home with his wife.

On most such Saturday evenings Freddie and Christine would drive northwards over the Thames together to arrive at the club at some time before midnight. On this particular evening Christine decided to wait for her son Donnie, who had borrowed her car, to return home – then, she said, she would follow Freddie to the club.

So that night Freddie drove himself alone in his Citroen car to Charing Cross Road, arriving around 11 p.m. He stopped and had a word with his doorman, Robert Deacon.

"How is it tonight?" he asked.

"So far it's pretty quiet," Deacon replied. "We've only got nine customers in at the moment."

Freddie said: "OK, I need a bit of kip, so I'll park around the back and have a nap in the car. Call me in about half an hour, will you?"

"Round the back" was in a dark, disused, deserted and

almost enclosed space called Goslett Yard, and if it seems unusual for a club owner to drive his car round to an empty car park and take a nap in it instead of going to his private office, it should be said at once that Freddie Mills habitually parked his car in Goslett Yard and habitually took a nap in it.

Promptly at 11.30 Robert Deacon went round to Goslett Yard to waken his boss. He found Freddie sitting on the back seat. The ex-world light-heavyweight champion was dead, shot through the eye. The murder weapon, a .22 rifle, was in the back of the car with him.

What had happened? That's where those close to Mills that night developed some sharply contrasting views. At the subsequent inquest the coroner – who rather curiously heard the case without the benefit of a jury – ruled that the ex-champion committed suicide.

This was despite the fact that Freddie, who was devoted to his wife and two daughters and who appeared to all intents and purposes to love life, left no note.

The gunshot wound from which he died, declared Professor Keith Simpson, the Home Office pathologist, was not inconsistent with Freddie shooting himself.

That wasn't a view shared by Leonard Pearce, a ballistics expert. He thought there was no way that Freddie could have pulled the trigger himself. Powerful evidence to support that view, it seems, was given by the ambulance man who took the body away. He said that when he reached into the car the rifle was in a position where it would have been impossible for Freddie to have shot himself. No one at the inquest ever suggested that the gun was touched before the ambulance man saw it, except Mrs. Mills who, after arriving at the club and being told her husband was "unwell," moved it to one side when she climbed in alongside Freddie to find out what was wrong with him.

Her view was unequivocal: the gun was by her husband's leg and could not have been put in that position if he had shot himself.

Even more powerful evidence was offered by the police fingerprint expert, who calmly told the coroner that there were no fingerprints on the gun. That would suggest that whoever was the last person to use it must have wiped it clean. That needless to say is a difficult thing for someone to do if they have just killed themselves.

But, declared the coroner, it had to be suicide.

Suicide? echoed his friends. By shooting himself through the eye with a .22 rifle? And by firing not one shot but two, since the first bullet had missed the pretty-hard-to-miss target and embedded itself in one of the car's doors?

To try to put the pieces together we need to study the time-table of events closely. Robert Deacon, as we have, seen, went to his boss at 11.30 p.m. and was unable to wake him. He would then have returned to the nite spot, around the corner, and told his boss, Andy Ho.

While this was going on, Mrs. Mills was still back at Denmark Hill, exasperated by the non-arrival of her son Donnie. He eventually showed up with her car just after midnight, and then volunteered to drive his mother to the night club. They left Denmark Hill at around 12.30, and at that time of the morning in those days traffic on the route, along the Walworth Road to Blackfriars and thence via The Strand to Charing Cross Road would have been very light. The journey could have been completed in less than 20 minutes, so we may assume that they arrived about 12.50, it now being Sunday.

A few minutes after their departure a Mrs. Budgeon, who was staying that weekend with the Mills family at their Denmark Hill house, received a phone call from Andy Ho, asking to speak to Mrs. Mills. When Mrs. Budgeon told him that Christine had already left for the club, Andy Ho reported that Freddie was outside in his car and unwell.

According to Mrs. Budgeon, she then told Ho: "Mrs. Mills will be there in a few minutes. Don't leave him in the car. Get him into the club," and he replied, "Yes, I will."

Andy Ho was on the pavement waiting for the arrival of

the boss's wife. He told her: "Freddie's ill. We can't wake him up. He's in his car."

Christine Mills and Donnie McCorkindale followed him round to Goslett Yard and peered into the car. Freddie was sitting in the back seat with the window open and no topcoat, despite it being a chilly night and despite the fact that he was still recovering from flu. Mrs. Mills got into the car beside him and noticed almost at once that he was dead – something, apparently, that neither Robert Deacon nor Andy Ho had noticed. His hands were on his knees and on the outside of his right leg was the .22 rifle. If her testimony was right, it clearly would have been impossible for Freddie Mills to have shot himself through the eye, put down the gun beside him, then put his hands on his knees before dying.

The biggest blank in all this is what happened between Robert Deacon's report to Andy Ho at 11.30 that his boss was "indisposed" and the arrival of Mrs. Mills and her son one hour and 20 minutes later. For that's what it was – a blank.

The biggest mystery in this case of mysteries concerns the .22 rifle. According to a *News of the World* journalist who investigated the shooting three years later, Freddie borrowed it from a Mrs. Mary Ronaldson, who was a life-long friend and ran a shooting gallery at Battersea Pleasure Gardens. She had 500 similar rifles.

She said: "Freddie said he wanted to attend a charity fête dressed as a cowboy. I handed him a rifle which had gone wrong and was due for repair. It was a semi-automatic self-loading rifle. You just pulled the trigger and didn't have to cock it after each shot. I didn't give him any ammunition but we found afterwards that he had taken three bullets from my home.

"He brought the rifle back two days after borrowing it saying the fête was cancelled. Then, on the Thursday, he called for it again. When I got it back after his death [Freddie died on the Saturday after this second borrowing of the gun] the rifle was working. How he, or somebody repaired it, I don't know."

Like so much of the Freddie Mills case, there appears to be conflict over dates concerning the rifle. The dates in the newspaper report are different from those given in evidence at the inquest, when Mrs. Ronaldson said the gun was first borrowed on the Tuesday of the week before Freddie's death, and returned to her on the following Thursday.

It was then, according to that evidence, borrowed again the next day, on Friday morning, with a promise to return it the following Saturday.

Freddie, she thought "had something on his mind and seemed to be wandering mentally, too. He asked how I spelled my name – and this after he had known me all his life."

She added: "I can't believe that he committed suicide. I can't understand why he left no notes. Another peculiar thing is that Freddie said he was scared of guns. He even asked my son to put the rifle in the car for him. He was frightened to touch it. Yet this was the instrument they say he chose to take his life with."

This testimony is nothing if not bizarre. If you want to commit suicide a .22 fairground rifle is about the last weapon you could choose for reliability. And if you want to dress up as a cowboy for a fete why choose a fairground rifle – especially if you're afraid of guns – when a toy gun would serve the purpose just as adequately?

But against that is Mrs. Ronaldson's assertion that Freddie took three bullets from her home, which takes some explaining.

And what happened in Freddie's life between the day when he returned the gun saying the fête was cancelled and the Thursday (or the Friday) when he borrowed it back? If the reason he wanted it for was suicide, had he postponed his own death for some unaccountable reason, and then later, when he took the gun again, decided to reinstate it?

Then again, would you commit suicide with a weapon

that terrified you to such an extent you didn't want to touch it?

Notwithstanding that, did he borrow it not for a cowboy fête but to threaten someone who was threatening him – someone with whom he had a rendezvous that night in Goslett Yard?

Just as intriguing as all this is the case of the first bullet – the one that he missed himself with. It was supposed to have been fired while he was sitting in the front seat, so that the rifle must have been virtually inches from him when he missed. But because he died in the back seat of the car, he must then have got out and climbed into the back and then shot himself in the eye. That would seem at least an extraordinary sequence of events.

All sorts of stories abounded at the time of Freddie's death to justify the theory of suicide.

One was that he was on the verge of bankruptcy. He was certainly less wealthy than he had been, but all the evidence was that he was a long way from bankruptcy. There were some unanswered questions in his financial accounts, concerning missing money, and there was a £4,000 bank loan taken up against the security of his house. These things suggest some money troubles, but Freddie Mills was not on his uppers when he died.

Another story suggested that he was a serial killer – the rapist-murderer in a series of West London killings where the victims' bodies were discovered naked. This wasn't seriously believed and was totally discounted by the police. Yet another story suggested just as wildly that he was a homosexual who feared being unmasked.

At the end of his life accountants discovered a big hole in his accounts – money gone missing with no explanation for it. It would not be difficult to imagine that it almost certainly went to protection racketeers, ruthless men who tore the amiable, naive ex-boxer apart financially, bleeding him like bloodsuckers.

Many businessmen paid protection money to gangsters in the Sixties while they could afford it. When they could no longer afford it there were few ways out for them.

If Freddie Mills was being forced to pay protection money and then decided he was paying too much, or wanted to negotiate some reduction in the "fee," because he couldn't afford what was being demanded, or if he refused to pay any more cash at all, he would not have had much sympathy from the extortioners.

He might have been asked for a chat, in some cosy out-of-the way place where no one could listen in. Not Freddie Mills's Nite Spot, with the customers in close proximity, but just round the corner in Goslett Yard. For this arranged rendezvous he took along the weapon, perhaps to threaten his persecutors, although that in itself would have been totally out of character.

There was a dialogue, perhaps, and then the weapon was turned on him. The racketeers would have been wearing gloves, which explains the lack of fingerprint evidence. Exactly what happened can never be known. What *is* known is that in the Sixties people in business who didn't pay the racketeers were frequently beaten up and sometimes murdered.

Among the several accounts of the mystery of Goslett Yard the best by far is a book called *The Strange Death of Freddie Mills*, by Bill Bavin, published by Howard Baker Books. Bavin was a long-time friend of Freddie, and he leaves no doubt in anyone's mind that his buddy was murdered by protection racketeers.

Asking his readers to imagine themselves as a gang boss engaged in extortion, Bavin writes:

"You decide that the Freddie Mills Nite Spot is ripe for trimming. And so handily situated you haven't got to send anyone too far for the collection of the 'pension', which was the particularly succinct description used in the Kray case.

"You find maybe that Freddie is a bit tougher than you imagined, and not prepared to be squeezed. So you start putting on the pressure."

Eventually, hypothesises Bavin, "you start drawing a

weekly or monthly subscription, call it what you will. Then, if business falls off a bit – and this is the conclusion to which everyone seems to have jumped, so it's admissible here – you find there is difficulty in collecting your agreed income from this source.

"So you suggest ways and means your victim can satisfy you – at least until business improves and he doesn't have to worry any more. You drain him step by step. After you are sure you've had everything out of his personal account, you show him how you can falsify other accounts to meet your demands.

"You tell him he can always mortgage his house. But when this is gone and when business hasn't improved to the tune of your demands, what do you do next?"

You're in a fix, according to Bavin, because you may be having trouble with other "clients" who are in difficulty with their payments to you. You have to give them an example of what happens when they don't pay up – and the best example of course is someone famous. Freddie Mills couldn't any longer afford to pay, so he was murdered as an example to other would-be non-payers in the nether world of Soho.

Bavin's hypothesis is backed by an amazing quotation which was passed on to him by Christine Mills. After her husband's death, she says she was told that other club owners in the area had been warned: "You'll see we mean business in a fortnight's time. Someone – a big name – is going to get done as an example to everybody that we aren't going to put up with being messed about."

Christine Mills told Bill Bavin that this warning was issued precisely two weeks before Freddie's death.

Bavin also reports a story from a criminal contact who said that he was "Paymaster" for a racketeering gang, and that the protection "wage bill" in London's West End central area was £2,000 a week.

Not all the gaps in the Freddie Mills mystery are plugged by Bavin's hypothesis. Nor does he over-speculate on what might have happened during Freddie's last few minutes on

Earth in the car at Goslett Yard.

Did, for instance, Freddie drive his car round to Goslett Yard, ostensibly to "take a nap" because he had a routine rendezvous with the racketeers? Did the meeting turn nasty, as perhaps they intended it too? Did the racketeers pick up the fairground rifle and use it on him? If so, that would be a strange thing for a professional criminal to do, because the last thing a pro would use to kill a man would be a fairground rifle.

In an intriguing epilogue to his investigation, Bavin says that when Donnie McCorkindale, Freddie's stepson, arrived at the club with Mrs. Mills on the night of the mystery death, Donnie took one look into the car, and ran back into the club crying out for someone to call an ambulance.

The ambulance duly arrived, and although this was clearly a case of violent death, involving a shooting (the ambulanceman would have been well aware of this because he actually moved the rifle when he got into the car) the body was taken away before the police arrived. "Even the family weren't told at first to which hospital."

Why, one wonders. For that single act alone broke all the rules of police investigation into a death in suspicious circumstances.

As for suicide, that surely, was a long way from being proven.

7

DOROTHY STRATTEN
Case of the Bunny Girl's Minder

There was nothing about their first encounter to suggest its dramatic sequel – nothing to indicate that the pushy would-be entrepreneur and the gauche blonde teenager would soon be making headlines.

Even the setting of that first meeting could not have been more commonplace: a Dairy Queen diner in Vancouver. He was a customer, fur-coated on that cold January evening in 1978. The tall, skinny 17-year-old whose fate was to become entwined with his was a waitress, decked out in a Dairy Queen red uniform.

Schoolgirl Dorothy Hoogstraten, or Stratten as she was to become, of Dutch parentage, had worked part-time at the diner since she was 14. She was shy, had little to say and was anything but sure of herself. Quite the last thing she expected was to attract the attention of a self-assured man of the world like Paul Snider, 27 and fast going places. At least, that was his image as he saw it.

Others viewed him differently. Men swiftly sized him up as a flashy, small-time smart operator whose achievements lagged far behind his aspirations. Most of them despised him for his showy womanising – his life seemed to be one long ego trip as he made the rounds of the Vancouver bars, always with a pretty girl on his arm.

He was with a woman companion when he called at the Dairy Queen, but that didn't stop him asking Dorothy

Hoogstraten her name as she took his order for a Strawberry Sundae Supreme. He followed this up later by phoning the Dairy Queen, asking for Dorothy. She wasn't on duty and her colleagues would not give him her phone number, so he left a message asking her to call him.

For Snider all this was routine. It was his practice to pursue just about every girl who caught his eye, and he was nothing if not persistent. In his mind's eye Dorothy was lined up to become yet another female for him to show off as he paraded the local bars and clubs. But while most men viewed him as a sleazy smoothie, girls tended to warm to him. He could be amusing, he had a generous nature and he was good-looking, if a trifle on the short side of five-foot-eight.

Dorothy's mother advised her not to call the number left by the persistent customer. So, daughters being what they usually are, Dorothy rejected that advice and picked up the phone. She already had a boy friend, but he was nothing special. She knew nothing of Paul Snider, but from what little she had seen of him he was certainly different from the callow youths who had dated her so far in her short life.

Snider asked her out. She was unwell at the time, and said no. He didn't give up. He waited and tried again. This time she said yes.

For that first date she dressed casually in a black top and grey trousers. He turned up in his black Datsun 240Z, kitted-out as usual in his fur-trimmed leather overcoat and dripping with jewellery – diamond rings, a gold bracelet, and the obligatory gold necklace with open-necked shirt... the uniform of Snider and his kind.

He did most of the talking. He probably had to, but to him it came easily. He took Dorothy to his apartment with its full-length mirrors, its big platform bed, its thick fur rugs and its balcony. The shy waitress was impressed. For her this was opulence.

He cooked dinner and then produced his guitar and played to her – he was not a bad musician. He sang her songs he said he had composed. He went on to tell her something of his wheeling and dealing as a businessman. He told her about the motor shows he promoted in both Vancouver and the United States. He described the California Truckin' and Cycle Show he organised in Los Angeles and the Motorcycle USA Show he staged at Long Beach.

What he did not mention, though, was that although some of his shows were money-spinners, the American ventures lost nearly all of the $100,000 contributed by a financial backer.

Paul Snider was primarily an ideas man and a bit of a butterfly, flitting from one project to another, never settling to anything for long, and always with an eye to the main chance. He claimed he originated wet T-shirt contests, and that he created sculptures out of metal-work. One of Vancouver's smart hotels displayed one of his pieces, and he opened his own shop-cum-gallery. It no longer existed – he had to close it when he withdrew money from the business to pay for a girl friend's debt. The girl had left him shortly afterwards, but Snider took that philosophically.

He figured that he was often simply unlucky. He blamed the failure of his Long Beach enterprise on a coinciding air show which kept people away. Although he lacked sustained application, while his enthusiasm for one of his projects lasted he threw himself into it heart and soul, working all hours. But somehow things never seemed to work out quite as he hoped.

As Snider told Dorothy all this, chatting up the naive teenager in his apartment, he gradually became aware that she was not quite the gawky kid she at first seemed. She had the open-faced beauty of innocence and she was still maturing and malleable – impressionable and ready to be moulded by the influence of a strong personality like Paul Snider's.

For him this was not new territory. He already had the reputation of being at best an exploiter of women, at worst, a pimp. For a time he lived with three girls who were suspected of being prostitutes. He drove them around, delivering them to clubs, and later collecting them. The police put him under surveillance, but he was never charged.

Dorothy didn't know what to make of him. Short on confidence and self-esteem, she wondered what such a personable man-about-town could see in the likes of her. The next night she went out with her regular boy friend, who now seemed dull and prosaic by comparison. But she had a bit of a conscience. She decided she wouldn't see Paul Snider again – not that she expected to hear from him. Such a sophisticated man, she thought, must have found her very dull company.

A day later, however, he phoned to say he would drive her to work. He duly picked her up and collected her again at the end of her shift. This gave her the opportunity to tell him about her steady boy friend. Snider kissed her good night, and that, she thought, was that.

But it wasn't. Anyone who knew Paul Snider could have told her that he was no quitter when he had a girl in his sights. The following evening he phoned again, asking her to go with him for a drive and a talk. They went to a local beauty spot where he parked and expounded his philosophy of life. He told her that happiness came from the heart, not the intellect. He said she should let how she felt, not how she thought she ought to feel, do her deciding. Her next date with her boy friend was her last. Her heart had plumped for Paul Snider.

On her 18th birthday, February 28th, 1978, her new lover gave her a diamond ring. And like a plant responding to water, she began to bud and bloom, her latent beauty glowing in response to Snider's affection. He also began to groom her, giving her the poise and confidence she so notably lacked, and encouraging her to stick up for herself at home. He was shocked to find that she even let her kid sister Louise dominate her.

But Paul Snider's courtship of Dorothy Hoogstraten was not unopposed. Dorothy's mother, whose husband had left her, was less than starry-eyed about men in general and about Snider in particular. She didn't like him. She thought him flashy and a bit of a crook.

Dorothy's boss also had no time for Snider. The burly biker who had the Dairy Queen franchise in Vancouver had known Snider for years and couldn't stand him. When he found the glib womaniser waiting for Dorothy at the diner he chucked him out. Dorothy had to make another choice. She packed in the part-time job.

To make her feel needed and to develop her self-confidence, Snider involved her in the organisation of his next motor show in March. In the autobiography she was later to begin writing she recalled how at that time she started to become aware that she was in love with Snider, but she had misgivings. She wondered whether she were really no more than his plaything.

She had good reason to wonder. Paul Snider still had another woman on a string. Her name was Bonne Amie, and she was a stripper.

Still, he seemed to be interested in Dorothy for one reason or another. He told her how beautiful she was, with a body that was now burgeoning into pin-up proportions, and he also put his money where his mouth was. He wanted a professional cameraman to photograph her nude; he was convinced that there could be big money in Dorothy's curves.

This was not the first time he had such an idea. In 1974 he took a blonde stripper to a professional photographer with the idea of getting her into *Playboy* magazine and becoming her manager. That venture came to nothing, but with Dorothy he sensed he had a better chance. With every month that passed she was growing into something special.

Snider's eagerness to get Dorothy into the magazine was given an edge by *Playboy's* launch of a nationwide search for its Silver Anniversary Playmate. The girl chosen would receive $25,000, and would then spend 1979 taking part in the magazine's promotional anniversary functions, as well as fulfilling a variety of public engagements.

During all this time Dorothy was still a high schoolgirl. Now she graduated – wearing a low-cut white dress chosen and bought by Snider – and started work for a communications conglomerate. When Snider suggested that she should have a go at becoming the 25th Anniversary Playmate she said yes – aware that the prize money alone represented more than her new job would pay in three years.

The cameraman he chose was Uwe Meyer, who, when he questioned her, was left in no doubt that she was relaxed and happy in the new career that her boy friend was planning for her.

But Snider wasn't too happy with Meyer's pictures, and turned to Ken Honey, whose work had already appeared in *Playboy*. Honey had little time for Snider – he was later to say that most people took an instant dislike to the thrusting young man whose handsome face seemed to wear a permanent smirk. He accepted the commission provided Dorothy's parent signed a document consenting to the session, as the girl was under 21.

Dorothy's mother was on holiday in Europe, and it was extremely unlikely that she would agree to her daughter baring all, even for the chance of $25,000. But Snider was not the sort of man to let a small snag like that stand in his way. He produced the necessary document complete with what he claimed was Mrs. Nelly Hoogstraten's signature.

Ken Honey was agreeably surprised and impressed when he turned up at Snider's apartment to meet the model he was to photograph. He was moved by her stunning looks and charmed by her naiveté. Afterwards he was to recall how she spoke of what she would do with the money if she won the coveted title. Her ideas centred on using the cash to help her family or Snider – she said nothing about helping herself.

A few nights later Dorothy was working as a cashier at one of Snider's motor shows when Ken Honey arrived with encouraging news. He had heard from *Playboy* – his pictures were well received, and the magazine wanted Dorothy to fly to Los Angeles straight away for more photography.

They had in fact already booked her flight – but there was no reservation for anyone accompanying her. Paul Snider, who had envisaged a lucrative career as Dorothy's manager, found that instead of being in the driving seat he had no seat at all.

This in fact was to be the pattern of Dorothy's upward progress from this time on. But at least his protégée was on her way. And he had another move up his sleeve. He planned to marry her.

In Los Angeles Dorothy's *Playboy* hosts were not disappointed by the girl who stepped off the plane from Canada. She was viewed as a strong contender for the Silver Anniversary title, and was whisked away for a session with the experienced centrefold photographer Mario Casili. He too was enchanted by the childish innocence of the teenager framed in his viewfinder. Far from "freezing" awkwardly as she stripped and posed, she clearly enjoyed the experience.

Taken to the *Playboy* guesthouse, she was undaunted by the celebrities surrounding her. But she was later to confess to going weak-kneed when she met Hugh Hefner, the magazine's founder-editor.

Two days later she returned to Vancouver, with a contract to return to Los Angeles the following month for a further fortnight's photography. While she was away Snider was on edge, anxious for news about how things were going. His anxiety was to intensify during Dorothy's subsequent periods away from him.

Now Dorothy was faced with some more decision-making. In order to fulfil the demands of Playboy she was having to take off a lot of time from her communications job. Where, she wondered, did her career lie? She decided to take the plunge and resigned from her job. Then she went off to Los Angeles again for three weeks rather than the originally scheduled fortnight.

They were weeks punctuated by phone call after phone call from Paul Snider, who was now becoming paranoiac. At the magazine's end of the line his persistent demands to speak to Mario Casili and others looking after Dorothy were regarded as a positive nuisance.

Snider undoubtedly sensed that his protégée was being drawn out of his orbit. Once again, he suspected, fate was conspiring against him just at the point when he should be making profits out of his successful launch of Dorothy.

She too was conscious of the gulf opening up between her and the man back home who set her on the road to possible stardom. She was increasingly aware of the differences between her heady new lifestyle in Los Angeles and the humdrum opportunities for advancement that were all that Snider could offer in Vancouver. Yet she felt she owed a debt to him, and this bothered her.

A month later, when she was back in Vancouver, Mario Casili arrived there to do some home-ground location photography. Snider's response was predictable. He hired a limousine for Dorothy and himself, telling Casili and his two helpers that they could follow behind with Ken Honey, who was also assisting in the assignment. This was the childish reaction of a man whose pride was hurt – and who deep down probably realised he did not have a lot to be proud of.

Slightly irritated, Casili instructed Honey to stop Dorothy's "minder" getting in the way. So Snider again found himself relegated to the sidelines, while his ego was demanding that he should be part of the action.

At last, in September, came the results of the Silver Anniversary Playmate contest. Dorothy after all had lost. But in competition with thousands of others she was the runner-up, selected to be Miss August, 1979, a triumph that netted her $10,000 plus a good chance of becoming Playmate of the Year for 1980.

Hoogstraten, though, was not thought to be a suitable name for a centrefold pin-up. She was henceforth to be called Dorothy Stratten.

Clasping each other jubilantly, Snider and Dorothy decided to get engaged. He bought her a big diamond ring and they moved together to Los Angeles. A few weeks after setting up home there, they rented out part of their house to a young doctor, Steve Cushner. Determined to become an actress, Dorothy went to drama classes, meeting and impressing the film director Peter Bogdanovich.

As Dorothy's fiancé, Snider was now admitted to functions at the *Playboy* guesthouse. But his face didn't fit, nor did his flashy clothes. What made him pass for a snappy dresser in Vancouver was 10 years behind the times in Los Angeles.

Everyone at *Playboy* considered him a parasite, and they were aghast when Dorothy married the man who was so tenaciously latching on to her. She herself was evidently not without misgivings. Weeks passed before she could bring herself to tell her mother that Snider was now her husband, and already she had left the matrimonial bed to sleep in another room.

Her $10,000 prize money was rapidly dwindling, and Snider was trying other methods to make ends meet. He pioneered male strippers at Chippendale's night-spot, promoted one of stuntman Evel Knievel's death-defying feats, commissioned a Dorothy Stratten poster which portrayed her provocatively on roller-skates, and applied his metal-work skills to producing benches for weight-lifters, following this up with benches complete with straps for customers who were into bondage.

He also tried unsuccessfully to get access to Dorothy's bank account. To bolster his flagging ego he bought himself some outrageously ostentatious jewellery.

Dorothy had the good sense to put her career in the hands of a professional management agency, and between attending acting classes and angling for film parts she worked at night as a bunny girl at the *Playboy* club.

As her dispirited husband became increasingly difficult, she frequently appeared red-eyed from crying. A *Playboy* executive bought her a puppy to cheer her up, but within days it was dead. Dorothy believed that Snider had poisoned her pet, jealous of the affection she showed it.

The couple were entertaining two friends when the conversation turned to wives deserting their husbands. Dorothy said she would never leave Paul. One of the friends asked why.

"Because he would kill me," she replied.

"Yeah," Snider confirmed. He didn't seem to be joking.

He hit rock bottom as an ideas man when came up with the notion of putting a full-page advertisement in the *Los Angeles Times* offering the secret of how to become a millionaire on receipt of $35. Only then would the secret of attaining millionaire status be sent to them – by which time, with a little luck, Snider would be a millionaire.

Things started coming good for Dorothy at last when she landed a key role in Bogdanovich's new movie, *They All Laughed*. At the same time, though, things started getting worse for Snider. He was seeing less and less of his glamorous wife, as the film was being shot in New York. He didn't know that Dorothy was now Peter Bogdanovich's mistress until a mutual friend inadvertently spilled the beans when she phoned Snider by mistake.

The friend confused the number with that of someone else, and without preamble launched into an account of the affair before she realised that it was the cuckolded husband on the other end of the line.

Dorothy Stratten had already drifted so far apart from Snider, however, that the news may not have come to him as a total surprise. He had lost his hold over her, and this fresh development merely reinforced the extent of that. He must have known that he would never get Dorothy back after this.

But Dorothy's mother was marrying again, and in an effort to stage a comeback Snider went to Vancouver to be at the wedding. Before the ceremony began Dorothy told him there was no room for him in her limo, and asked him to follow on in a cab. Acquaintances who once despised Paul Snider now began to feel sorry for him. He had become a pathetic hanger-on.

June, 1980, brought him a letter from Dorothy. She was now Playmate of the Year, and she was through with playing with Paul. Her letter said she wanted to live apart from him.

He hired a lawyer in a bid to get some kind of financial cut out of the split-up, and it seemed that he even cherished a forlorn hope that Dorothy might change her mind and come back to him. To this end he persuaded her to see him to discuss details of their separation agreement.

They met at their Los Angeles home and, true to form, Snider took flowers and champagne and dressed up in a new suit. He turned on every ounce of his charm but got nowhere. Dorothy, by contrast, turned up dressed as casually as she did on their first date. They failed to reach a financial settlement and she departed without troubling to pick up his flowers.

Snider brooded. And bought a gun.

Dorothy Stratten was now fully committed to Peter Bogdanovich. Those in their circle said they were made for each other. The naive, impressionable Dorothy Hoogstraten had thought she was in love with the man who put her on the road to celebrity. But the more mature Dorothy Stratten was experiencing the real thing with the personable film-maker who was equally devoted to her.

Dorothy and her estranged husband fixed a further meeting to sort out their split, a date known only to themselves and Dorothy's sister Louise. The time was 10.30 a.m., the day Thursday, August 14th, 1980, the place their home.

On her way there Dorothy, now 20, called at her bank for $1,000, which was presumably for her husband. Not that he would have been content with that. He was pressing for her to set him up in a $185,000 house in North Hollywood.

The couple's two cars were still outside their home at 5 p.m. Every now and then Snider's phone rang and went unanswered. Their tenant, the young doctor Steve

Cushner, came home an hour later. and made himself a meal. At 11 p.m. a perturbed Cushner went to Snider's bedroom and knocked. There was no response, so he opened the door.

As a doctor he instantly recognised the substance spattered all over the room. It was brain material – the brains of the once beautiful Dorothy Stratten, who lay partly on the bed, partly on the floor, with half her face blown away. And the brains of her husband, who was pitched forward on his face with his skull demolished by the shotgun which lay underneath him.

Tresses of Dorothy's blonde hair were in his hands. The two were both naked, and it seemed that Snider had forced the Playmate of the Year to have sex with him, binding her to his bondage bench in the process.

Then, at around 1 p.m., he shot her as she sat on the bed, putting the shotgun to his own right temple half an hour later. Dorothy must have raised a hand to her face in self-defence, for her index finger was shot away.

Those closest to the tragedy were devastated. Peter Bogdanovich risked bankruptcy endeavouring to distribute *They All Laughed*, his tribute to the girl he wanted to make his wife. She was buried near the grave of Marilyn Monroe, and nine years later Bogdanovich married her sister. No more centrefolds were shot by Mario Casili for *Playboy*.

Paul Snider's few intimate friends said he destroyed Dorothy because she destroyed him by breaking his heart. But, true to form, when he bought the murder weapon he haggled over the price...

8

SPENCER PERCEVAL
Murder of a British Prime Minister

Imagine the consternation that would be caused, the headlines and the hysteria that would sweep across the world, if a British Prime Minister were to be murdered in the House of Commons. Yet it happened once before – and today hardly anyone remembers the Prime Minister's name.

He was Spencer Perceval, and many people thought he was doing rather a good job as Tory Prime Minister until the afternoon of May 11th, 1812, when he was gunned down as he entered the lobby of the House of Commons at the age of 50.

No one, least of all Perceval himself, would have reckoned on his chances of ever reaching such dizzy political heights when he set out to earn his living as a young man. Although he was the second son of an earl, that didn't mean anything in the second half of the eighteenth century, for first sons usually inherited everything and anyone who came after them usually got a good education and nothing else.

Perceval's good education took him to Harrow and then to Cambridge University and law school. But when he married at the age of 38 the well-to-do family of his bride, Mary Wilson, were very much against the union on account of his poverty, and the bride, we are told, went to the altar "only dressed in her riding-habit."

Some of the in-laws' hostility might have been brought about by his physical appearance, as much as his empty purse. He was thin, pale and short. A cabinet minister later nicknamed him "Little P." But fellow-lawyers liked him. They described him as calm, sincere, affectionate, intensely religious "and of a severe and upright morality."

But already Perceval was revealing himself as the kind of law-maker he would one day become in Parliament. He didn't like change. He wanted to uphold all the old ways and traditions of high birth and privilege which were beginning to hang like rocks around the neck of John Bull. He believed passionately in the rich man in his castle and the poor man at his gate as being the work of Divine Providence, with which no man should interfere. He thought lords and gentlemen should rule the less fortunate, and was implacably opposed to parliamentary reform, which in due course could not be erased from the agenda despite die-hards like Perceval.

The Percevals had five children in the first six years of their marriage, and he had to work hard to make both ends meet. But a political pamphlet he wrote came to the attention of Prime Minister William Pitt, who was sufficiently impressed by it to propose a political career for the struggling lawyer.

Perceval demurred – if life was tough on a lawyer's salary, he reasoned, it would be probably even tougher on a politician's salary, and the wrong move would imperil his family's prospects for all time.

The letter he wrote back to Pitt impressed the Prime Minister even more. "I could not accept any terms you offer me because I feel they would be too great for any service I could render to the public," he said.

Pitt, who was a tough politician, knew how rare it was to find at that time so much dignity, so much modesty and so much consideration for the public interest, and he did not forget it.

These were momentous times for England. Napoleon Bonaparte was on his way to supreme power in Paris, and although Nelson had command of the seas English people feared a French invasion at any moment. Workers of the new industrial age were living in grinding poverty; the King, George III, was going mad, and his son, the Prince of Wales, who was to become Prince Regent, was discrediting the monarchy with his debauchery.

This was hardly the scenario in which to introduce a man who disliked change, for change was what Britain desperately needed. Yet things happened swiftly for Spencer Perceval. Three months after that letter to Pitt he was elected MP for Northampton. He made a big impression on his party leader, for when Pitt was obliged to fight a duel he was asked who he thought should succeed him if he were killed.

He reflected, then said, "I think Mr. Perceval is the most competent person."

Pitt survived the duel and Perceval became Solicitor General, then Attorney General. When Pitt died Perceval took over as leader of the Tory opposition in the House of Commons. Even a brush with the arrogant Prince of Wales, who heartily disliked this new man, failed to dent his prospects.

When the Tories were returned to government Perceval became Chancellor of the Exchequer in the administration of the Duke of Portland. There were seven future Prime Ministers in the Cabinet: Perceval, Liverpool, Canning, Robinson, (the future Viscount Goderich), Wellesley (the future Duke of Wellington), Peel and Palmerston. But its chief, the ageing Duke of Portland, was failing in health and exercised little control. When the Duke finally resigned in September, 1809, Perceval became Prime Minister in October.

The following year the madness of King George made a Regency Bill necessary. This was a difficult measure to push through Parliament because the Prince of Wales wanted more power than the government would give him. Perceval spoke with great courage and independence against letting the Prince have too much of his own way, though he had most of the royal family against him. The government won the day, and when the Prince became Regent, perhaps conscious of the feeling in the country, he decided to continue with Perceval's government in office.

By the beginning of 1812 – by which time he was the father of no fewer than 12 children – Perceval was recognised as an able Prime Minister and a resolute leader. But what he did not know was that right there under his nose a regular visitor to the House of Commons' Strangers' Gallery was taking a chilling interest in him.

In some ways John Bellingham was a bit like Spencer Perceval. He was short and slim, a man of reserve and deliberate silences. Born in St. Neots, he had suddenly walked away from his wife Mary and their three young children and moved to lodgings in London. Mary Bellingham probably sighed with relief at that, for she knew him as a pretty poor father.

Bellingham, who was a bankrupt and had recently been discharged from prison, took a bachelor flat in the Gray's Inn district and passed his time visiting picture galleries and museums. Sometimes too he spent hours in solitary reflection in churches. Before long his wanderings took him to the House of Commons, and soon his attendances in the Strangers' Gallery were so frequent that the usher almost kept his seat there reserved for him.

Whenever occasion offered, he would sit there and study Prime Minister Perceval through a pair of opera glasses. For the rest of the public in the gallery he seemed harmless enough. They were not to know that his father died insane, that he was developing paranoia that required a focusing point, and that Spencer Perceval provided it.

Bellingham's grievance was actually created in Russia, which in that year of 1812 was to bear the brunt of Napoleon's determination to make a dream of empire come true. Some time before the Retreat from Moscow, Bellingham travelled to the Russian port of Archangel, near the Artic Circle.

Although the facts of the case are not clear, he was

arrested there for dishonesty on a charge laid by someone named Solomon van Brienen. Russian justice in those days was not fast moving, so it was some time before the case was brought to court.

The long wait, which he had to spend in a filthy, rat-infested jail, infuriated the Briton. He began writing petitions to the Russian authorities and to the British ambassador demanding his release as a falsely accused person.

His impassioned pleas produced only studied in-difference, so when he was finally brought to court, found not guilty and released, he was harbouring a deep grudge against his accusers. And he wouldn't let it go. He went to St. Petersburg where he attempted to gain access to the British ambassador, Lord Granville Leveson-Gower, who had him thrown out.

After that he became such a nuisance pestering the Russian authorities for compensation for wrongful arrest that they put him back in jail. Only when his pockets were empty and a convenient ship arrived that could transport him back to England was he released.

Still Bellingham wouldn't let go his hold on his grudge. In England he began a fresh round of petitions, and pretty soon all he had gained was a reputation as a bore. Undaunted, he even sent a petition to the Prince Regent. He received a polite but formal reply, to the effect that His Royal Highness was unable to do anything personally in the matter.

He got the same sort of response from the Privy Council, and when he wrote to Prime Minister Perceval, who could never have guessed what that letter would lead to, he was again cold-shouldered. Still undaunted, he became a frequent caller at the doors of MPs and anyone else he thought might be helpful in procuring what he regarded as justice for John Bellingham.

When his literary and physical energies began to flag, Bellingham wrote flowery letters to his wife, explaining his hopes, which included receiving a considerable sum in compensation so that he could return to Liverpool, where his family were now living, and take his parental responsibilities more seriously. What Mrs. Bellingham thought of these outpourings can only be imagined.

In May, 1812, Bellingham wrote one of his supplications to a Bow Street magistrate, who read it and threw it away.

But that letter contained a clue to the changing state and condition of the writer's upset mind. For the first time he mentioned feeling that he might be compelled to administer justice himself.

The Bow Street magistrate could be pardoned for believing that the letter-writer was a crank. But the threat it contained suggested that this was a dangerous crank.

Simple inquiry would have uncovered evidence that Bellingham had recently acquired two pistols. On the afternoon of May 11th he loaded them both, carefully measuring the charge of powder for each, and ramming home the ball-shot. He put one into each of his two inside pockets in his coat. Into one of the outside pockets he put a collection of documents about his grievances which he had carried backwards and forwards many times across London, and into the other he put his opera glasses.

Then he put on the coat with its bulging pockets to walk through the spring sunshine from Gray's Inn to King Street, St. James's. From there he turned into the European Museum, long since replaced by Christie's auction rooms.

He spent some time gazing at the objects in the museum and then set out for Westminster. In the lobby of the House of Commons he stopped and took off his hat. Several people who passed him thought that he appeared to be waiting for someone. He was in fact waiting for the Prime Minister to appear.

One person who saw him there was a Scottish writer named William Jerdan, who was later to recall what he witnessed that afternoon just before 5 p.m.

The House was in committee that day and it was later than usual before the Prime Minister got away. He entered

Marilyn Monroe and President
John Kennedy. For him the risk
seemed to add spice to the affair.
Chapter 1

Gianni Versace, and right his assassin, Andrew Cunanan.
Chapter 2

Sal Mineo. Destined to come to a sticky end.
Chapter 3

John Lennon (above) signing an autograph for Mark Chapman (right) just hours before Chapman murdered the former Beatle. *Chapter 4*

Vicki Morgan. In the 1980 US election campaign she was George Bush's driver and guide. *Chapter 5*

Dorothy Stratten and Paul Snider. The case of the bunny girl and her minder.
Chapter 7

Freddie Mills. The rifle was in a position where it would have been impossible for Freddie to have shot himself.
Chapter 6

Left, John Bellingham and below, Prime Minister Spencer Perceval being shot dead in the lobby of the House of Commons.
Chapter 8

George Reeves. Who put a live bullet in Superman's gun?
Chapter 9

Below, Hollywood's "Ice Cream Blonde" Thelma Todd and left, dead in her car. *Chapter 10*

Mahatma Gandhi. A violent end for a man of peace. *Chapter 11*

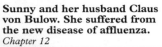
Sunny and her husband Claus von Bulow. She suffered from the new disease of affluenza. *Chapter 12*

Bob Crane, TV's Colonel Hogan. Sex, blue movies and murder. *Chapter 13*

Ramon Novarro. A shocking death for cinema's great Latin Lover. *Chapter 14*

Below, Leon Trotsky and right, the desk he sat at when attacked. *Chapter 15*

Gig Young. "You play a loser long enough...you end up a loser." *Chapter 16*

Marvin Gaye. "If he found happiness, he always found a way to lose it." *Chapter 17*

the lobby and paused to look round before crossing the floor. That was when Bellingham's right hand jerked one of the pistols from his inside pocket.

There was a mere frozen moment of realisation of what was happening as the Rt. Hon. Spencer Perceval stared at the little round iron mouth of the pistol pointing at his chest. For a split second two men born at opposite ends of the social structure, both of them introverts, small, and insignificant in appearance, stared at each other. Then the gun exploded and the ball smashed into the Prime Minister's heart. He cried out, lurched forward and was already dead when his body collapsed on the floor.

Standing some yards away, William Jerdan stood rooted to the spot with horror, switching his gaze from the dead man to his killer, who was now staggering to a seat and dropping down, his shoulders shaking violently.

The sound of the pistol shot brought people running into the lobby. One of them was Liverpool MP General Isaac Gascoyne, to whom Bellingham had written on many occasions. Gascoyne immediately recognised the shivering man holding a discharged pistol and seized him.

"Are you the murderer?" he demanded.

"I am that unfortunate man," Bellingham replied stiffly.

From behind the general someone shouted, "Villain! How could you destroy so good a man and make a family of 12 children orphans?"

Bellingham looked over the general's shoulder at the speaker, then replied in a low voice, "I am sorry for it."

They sounded like stilted lines in a bad play but in that historic place they carried terrible conviction. Bellingham was very pale, momentarily shaken into awareness of what he had done. Although that impact appeared to fade when he was arrested, Jerdan the writer noted that the killer's face "wore the hue of the grave, blue and cadaverous."

He wrote immediately afterwards: "Drops of sweat ran down his forehead, and from the bottom of his chest to his throat rose and fell with almost every breath a spasmodic action, as if something were choking him. The miserable wretch repeatedly struck his chest with the palm of his hand to abate the sensation, but it refused to be repressed."

An escort of cavalry took the arrested man to a cell in Newgate Prison, where almost the first task undertaken by the compulsive letter-writer was this message to his landlady:

"Dear Madam, Yesterday midnight I was escorted to this neighbourhood by a noble troop of Light Horse and delivered into the care of Mr. Newman as a State prisoner first class. For eight years I have never found my mind so tranquil as since this melancholy but necessary catastrophe, as the merits or demerits of my peculiar case must now be regularly unfolded in a criminal court of justice to ascertain the guilty party by a jury of my country.

"I have to request the favour of you to send me three or four shirts, some cravats, handkerchiefs, night-caps, socks, etc., together with soap, toothbrush, and every other trifle that presents itself which you think I may have occasion for, and enclose them in my leather trunk. The key please to send sealed. Which will much oblige, dear madam, your very obedient servant, John Bellingham.

"P.S. To the above please add the prayer book."

All Britain was aghast at the killing, news of which spread across the land within 24 hours. Bellingham was probably the most unaffected emotionally, while the Prime Minister underwent a change from somewhat neglected party leader into near-hero just by the manner of his death.

Parliament showed its feelings by voting a substantial sum for their dead leader's widow and children in the knowledge that Perceval was never a wealthy man. The playwright Richard Brinsley Sheridan, who penned *The School for Scandal* and *The Rivals*, and who was himself an MP, delivered an oration in Stafford Town Hall in which he declared that Perceval was "a man who in his public life was pure in his intentions and purposes, and in his private life possessed of every quality calculated to win affection and command respect."

Meanwhile Bellingham was visited in his cell by the City

of London's sheriffs. He told them that he shot the Prime Minister because he was being refused justice.

"Had I shot him out of malice I would have been worse than a brute," he said. "It was the minister, not the man, who led me to do it. If there were a million lives to lose I would have done the same thing."

Justice was anything but wayward in Regency England. Bellingham was brought to trial at the Old Bailey on Friday morning, May 15th, and already by seven o'clock huge crowds thronged Holborn, Fleet Street and Ludgate Circus. The Old Bailey doorkeepers were charging a guinea for a seat inside; after another seven hours they raised the price to three guineas.

The trial was presided over by the Lord Chief Justice who had with him on the Bench the Lord Mayor, the Recorder of London, the Duke of Clarence, the Marquis of Wellesley, and General Gascoyne. The marquis was a member of Perceval's cabinet and the general, as we have seen, was an MP and witness to the shooting, so Bellingham might have had a good point if he had complained that in the circumstances he wasn't going to get a fair trial.

They all stared at the placid figure in the dock in his snuff-coloured coat, apparently unruffled by all the stir he had caused.

His counsel began by asking for a postponement on the grounds that there had been no time to summon witnesses from Liverpool. This was rejected, and when the Attorney General finished presenting the evidence the prisoner was asked if he had anything to say in his defence.

"My papers have all been taken from me," he told the court. "It is therefore impossible for me to present my justification."

The Attorney General produced the confiscated papers and handed them to the prisoner. Bellingham at once launched into a résumé of his treatment in Russia and the subsequent refusal of everyone to whom he appealed for help.

He was nothing if not dramatic. Gripping the rail of the dock he cried out, "My God! My God! What heart could bear such excruciating tortures without bursting with indignation at treatment so diametrically opposed to justice and humanity? Was it possible for me to regard the actions of the ambassador and council of my own country with any other feeling than detestation and horror?"

The bland looks of those on the Bench suggested that if there were an answer to that question they weren't interested in hearing it. Their looks seemed to change to something resembling agreement with Bellingham when he went on: "When I consider the amiable character and universally admired virtues of Mr. Perceval, I admit that if I had murdered him in a cool and unjustified manner I should not deserve to live another moment in this world."

Nonetheless, he was confident he could justify everything he had done and weather the storm that awaited him.

He was certainly right about the storm, although his confidence was totally misplaced, particularly when he boomed out: "Had I met Lord Leveson-Gower, the British ambassador, that day in Russia, instead of Mr. Perceval, he is the man who would have received the ball!"

His plea went on until his voice was droning out such advice to the future as, "I can only trust that this lesson will operate as a warning to future ministers and lead them to do the thing that is right."

He ended: "Sooner than go on suffering as I have done for eight years, I would consider five hundred deaths preferable!"

So saying he leaned forward to speak to his counsel, who much to his astonishment was advised by Bellingham to contact Mrs. Bellingham in Liverpool at once with the happy news of her husband's acquittal.

John Bellingham was clearly living in a world of his own – a world which none of his audience that day understood. The bemused and bewildered counsel for the defence was able to do nothing for his client, save to listen with a look of growing anguish on his face.

The jury received their instructions from the Bench. It was not really necessary for them to retire to consider their verdict, but, completely overawed by the occasion, they chose to do so. Bellingham regarded their absence with happy composure, for he was a man for whom reality had ceased to exist.

Very soon after the jury's departure some muttering and fidgeting in the crowded courtroom signalled their return. The foreman stood to deliver his verdict: "Guilty."

That single word at last registered in John Bellingham's confused brain. It was like setting a match to tinder. He was suddenly a man bursting with indignation and incredulity.

But for the first time since entering the dock he was tongue-tied. The verdict was a clear inversion of all he had seen in such clear mental perspective. For him it was a denial of the justice he was seeking and so confidently anticipated receiving.

He was prodded into standing while the Recorder intoned the death sentence. Solemnly Bellingham bowed to the Bench.

As a convicted murderer he was placed in irons and his diet reduced to bread and water. He was due to die within 48 hours – that would be one week exactly after the murder. Most of these last few hours were taken up with visits from clergymen trying to bring peace to a soul in torment.

Perhaps his one course of solace in those critical hours, when his unbalanced mind finally came to terms with reality, was a return to letter-writing.

On the night of Sunday, May 17th, he wrote his last letter. It was to his wife:

"My blessed Mary. – It rejoiced me beyond measure to hear that you are likely to be well provided for. I am sure the public at large will participate in and mitigate your sorrows. I assure you, my love, that my sincerest endeavours have ever been directed to your welfare. As we shall not meet any more in this world, I sincerely hope we shall do so in the world to come.

"With the purest intentions, it has always been my misfortune to be thwarted, misrepresented, and ill-used in life. But we feel a happy prospect of compensation in a speedy translation to the eternal. It is not possible to feel more placid or calm than I feel, and nine hours more will waft me to those happy shores where bliss is without alloy. Yours, ever affectionate. – J.B.

"P.S. Mr. Ford will forward you my watch and prayer book, with a guinea. Once more, God be with you, my sweet Mary. The public sympathise much with me, but I have been called upon to play an anxious card in life."

On Monday morning, he rose from his bunk at six o'clock, washed, dressed, and read his prayer book. He paused briefly as he entered the prison yard. As he moved across the yard a sudden gust of wind blew in his face.

"Ah, it rains heavily," he was heard to observe, as though taking satisfaction from the change in the weather. He halted to have the irons removed from his hands and legs and was then escorted to where the sheriffs were waiting. He was asked if he had a confederate in planning the shooting and the suggestion brought his head up with a jerk.

"Certainly not!" he snapped indignantly.

"Then it was your own affair for personal resentment?" he was pressed by an anxious official.

Some warmth crept into Bellingham's voice as he replied: "I bear no resentment to Mr. Perceval as a man. But I was referred from minister to minister, from office to office, and at last refused redress for my grievance.

"It was my own sufferings that caused the melancholy event. I hope it may be a warning to future ministers to attend to the requests of those who suffer oppression. I am sorry for the sufferings I have caused to Mr. Perceval's family and friends."

It was a gallows speech, still voicing an unshakeable conviction. An enormous crowd had gathered to gawk. As the clock of St. Sepulchre's began striking eight, they watched silently as the hangman placed the noose over Bellingham's head. The clock was still striking as the tied body was released and the condemned man swung in a plunging dive.

Rain was still falling as the people shuffled away. They must have wondered why anyone should want to die for such a senseless murder.

How insane was John Bellingham? Undoubtedly he shared his father's weakness of intellect. The tragedy was that the truth of his family mental illness was not released until after his death.

Sir Richard Westmacott, the celebrated Victorian sculptor, recorded for posterity the death of the 50-year-old Prime Minister with a realistic monument depicting the murder. It can still be seen in Westminster Abbey.

Did Britain lose a great Prime Minister? There are mixed views about that. A hundred years after Perceval's murder, the historian Clive Bigham summed him up: "He was a man of limited views and of dogged tenacity, but an honest and able minister, whose private views strengthened and confirmed his conservatism. It may well be that his martyrdom was the salvation of his political reputation."

9

GEORGE REEVES
Who put a Live Bullet in Superman's Gun?

The role of Superman has been a disastrous one for Hollywood. The first Superman, George Reeves, came to a mysterious and untimely death. The name of the second, Christopher Reeve, was oddly similar, and he too was the victim of a tragic accident, paralysed after a fall from a horse.

It is to the first Superman, George Reeves, that we now direct our thoughts, turning back the clock to the evening of June 16th, 1959, and the last hour in Superman's life.

That evening Reeves, famed world-wide for his starring role in the TV series, was entertaining two guests at his Beverly Hills home. They were Lenore Lemmon, his attractive but fiery fiancée, and Robert Condon, a journalist.

Lenore served dinner at about 6.30. After the meal the three sat drinking wine and spirits as they watched television. At midnight they went to bed.

About an hour later they were roused by someone pounding on the front door. The callers were two of Reeves's and Lenore's friends, apparently oblivious of the hour. Or maybe the night was still young for them. George Reeves was well known for keeping open house, so the two friends, William Bliss and Carol Von Ronkel, had decided to drop by on their way to wherever they were going.

But visitors weren't quite so welcome after midnight, as

Reeves told them when he appeared in a bathrobe after Lenore got up to let them in.

No one is at their best when woken within an hour of nodding off, especially after a heavy drinking session, and that night Reeves was a less than gracious host. But Lenore soon soothed his ruffled temper sufficiently for him to join the late-night visitors for a night-cap before he stumped off back to bed.

"He's just sulking," Lenore explained, as if trying to excuse him. "He'll probably go up to his room and shoot himself."

Reeves's friends shared the joke. Faking suicide by putting a gun to his head and squeezing the trigger was his favourite party trick when drunk, the gun containing just a blank. So when a shot rang out it seemed that George was at it again, too intoxicated to realise he hadn't an audience.

But his guests were no more sober than Reeves himself, and they were wrong about that shot. Upstairs he was sprawled on his bed, lying on his back. A bullet had ploughed through his head. As the newspapers were soon to announce, Superman was dead.

The circumstances, said the Beverly Hills police department, "indicated suicide." Which was what the Hollywood establishment wanted to hear. Anything else would have created embarrassing waves for one or two at the top.

Few, however, believed that George Reeves had taken his own life. Suicides simply didn't happen like that, as those familiar with sudden death were quick to point out. And besides, Reeves had a lot to live for. He was far from depressed. He had everything going for him in a flourishing career. The only cloud on his horizon concerned some menacing phone calls which he was continually receiving. Calls that threatened his life...

Nothing added up. The police claimed that Reeves went up to his bedroom, stuck the pistol in his right ear and pulled the trigger. But private investigators called in by the film star's mother found that there were no powder burns on Reeves's face. That meant that the gun was fired at least 18 inches from his head. People who shoot themselves almost invariably put the weapon to their head. They do not hold it away at arm's length.

The bullet lodged in the bedroom ceiling. That indicated that the victim's head was twisted, an unlikely posture for a suicide.

Furthermore, the police said that in shooting himself in the head, Reeves pulled the trigger with his right hand. That, of course, was to be expected of a right-handed man. Except that Reeves's right hand was temporarily disabled, the result of an incident in which his car struck a wall after hitting an oil slick. A newspaper had reported: "Superman fainted after the crash!"

In Los Angeles Superior Court, Reeves had filed a personal injury claim seeking half a million dollars in damages. Would he really have used that injured hand to fire a gun known to have a hefty kick?

Fingerprints, of course, might have settled any argument about who held the gun. But the police mysteriously failed to check for any. It was difficult to get a coherent account from others in the house, they said, because they were all so drunk.

Everyone who knew George Reeves insisted that he was not the suicidal type. With one voice they rejected the suicide theory, pointing out that he was on a high and his prospects were never better. "I never saw him happier," said the film star Alan Ladd. This was confirmed by Reeves's mother, who spoke to him only hours before he died. He was in great spirits, she said.

His first marriage ended in divorce after nine years. Now, 10 years later, he had found Lenore, and they were soon to wed.

Reeves had a long, lean period in which he played in only a few major films, but never as the star. They included *Gone with the Wind*, *From Here to Eternity*, and the Victor Mature – Hedy Lamarr version of *Samson and Delilah*.

But his Superman role made him a celebrity. The

television films were being screened in 30 countries, and he even had a fan letter from the Emperor of Japan.

During his career Reeves had done a lot of boxing, suffering a broken nose no fewer than nine times. His fame as Superman was bringing him lucrative spin-offs – personal appearances that were soon to climax with one particular event which zoomed in on his success as a boxer.

This was to be an exhibition match with Archie Moore, the light-heavyweight boxing champion, and it was an event Reeves was eagerly anticipating. It was the reason that the writer Robert Condon was staying with him, for Condon was preparing an article previewing the big occasion.

After that Reeves and Lenore were to honeymoon in Spain, prior to six weeks in Australia promoting the launch there of the Superman television series with personal appearances. That trip alone would put at least $20,000 in Reeves's pocket, and his forthcoming schedule for that year ended up with being back in Hollywood to direct a movie in which he was to star.

Lined up with all this there were more instalments of the Superman series, coupled with a new contract reflecting the higher fees he was now able to command.

Those were not the kind of prospects that went with suicide. They promised a rosy future for a man for whom everything was coming good.

But if George Reeves did not shoot himself, who did? His business manager Arthur Weissman thought he knew the answer. Superman did indeed pull the trigger, but he expected nothing more than a detonation of a blank. Whenever he played that drunken party trick, he held the gun far enough away to avoid getting scorched – hence the absence of powder burns.

But someone replaced the blank with a live round. And Weissman thought he knew who was responsible for that – although 30 years were to pass before he felt safe enough to name them. That person was a Hollywood mogul who was not only noted for his practical jokes – he had also been cuckolded by George Reeves.

Edgar J. Mannix was a former vice-president of Metro-Goldwyn-Mayer. His glamorous wife Toni was 25 years his junior, and in Hollywood her romance with Reeves was an open secret. It had endured for some years, and she was crazy about him. On his last birthday she had given him a Jaguar car.

But the man who played Superman was also "Superlover," with many other conquests, and his affair with Toni Mannix ended abruptly when he announced his engagement to Lenore, a feisty brunette socialite who had quite a track record herself. She was once thrown out of the Stork Club in New York for brawling with a woman competing with her for another man.

Toni, by all accounts, was furious to find herself suddenly supplanted by the woman Reeves was to marry. "I'll get even with you if it's the last thing I do," she was said to have told him during one of the countless hourly calls she put through to his home.

It was she who Reeves suspected was behind the threatening phone calls he had been getting for the past two months – up to 20 a day, and more often than not late at night, to ensure he had a troubled sleep. He would pick up his phone, often only to hear the receiver being replaced at the other end of the line. The last such call came just a couple of hours before he was shot.

His number was ex-directory, so the caller was clearly close to someone who had been close to him. And that someone instigating the calls if not actually making them, he told Beverly Hills police, was Toni Mannix. The calls were sufficiently disturbing for him to report them also to the Los Angeles County district attorney.

Following up Reeves's claims, investigators found that Toni too was receiving threats over the phone. That shifted the finger of suspicion to point at the cuckolded husband, Eddie Mannix.

And that wasn't all. In recent months Reeves had experienced three narrow escapes from death on the road.

First his car was mangled between two lorries. Then he had to leap out of the path of a speeding car heading straight for him. Next his brakes failed totally while he was driving along a hazardous lane. Someone, it seemed, had drained the car's brake fluid. That was the verdict of a mechanic who examined the car and said he could offer no other explanation since there was nothing else wrong with the hydraulics.

In Weissman's view all this added up to just one thing: that someone was trying to kill Superman. And Eddie Mannix, humiliated by Reeves's brazen affair with Toni, had a motive, together with the power, money and know how to put out a death contract on the Casanova he had every reason to hate.

For someone like Mannix, hiring hit-men to manoeuvre two lorries to sandwich a car would be no problem. The same thing applied to Reeves's other near-misses on the road – they would have been easy to set up, at a price. Similarly, entering the victim's home and replacing the blank in his gun with a bullet would have presented no great difficulty, for Mannix's wife had a key to the house. Then all the killer would have to do was wait for George Reeves to play his little game and obligingly shoot himself.

And that, Weissman believed, was precisely what had happened.

Investigators hired by Reeves's mother, though, had a different theory. They believed that an intruder was in Reeves's bedroom when the intoxicated film star reeled in and saw him. Reeves went for his German Luger, and in the ensuing scuffle the worse-for-wear actor was overpowered and shot with his own gun, the killer then fleeing the house.

But this scenario was less than plausible. Would an intruder – whether a hit-man or a burglar – have chosen a night when there were so many people in the house?

The victim's mother called off her investigation once it was shown to her satisfaction that his death was no suicide. She wasn't so interested in who killed him. She only wanted to establish that her boy hadn't taken his own life.

Her relationship with her son had always been a peculiar one in which she was overwhelmingly possessive. It was not until he was in the US Army that he discovered his actual birthday and that he was illegitimate. She continued to be so possessive that for a spell of nearly 10 years he refused to speak to her.

She was also protective, having tried in vain to quash his youthful enthusiasm for boxing. In an effort to "cure" him once and for all of his fondness for the ring, she once fixed it so that he found himself facing a massive mauler who gave him a thorough thrashing. Reeves took it like a man, and it served only to sharpen his appetite for the noble art.

A photograph of her George stood on his mother's piano, and in front of it a candle burned, an "eternal flame." That was when he was in his thirties, still going places, still turning heads.

If Eddie Mannix was the man behind George Reeves's shooting, he didn't enjoy his revenge for long. Within four years he himself was dead.

His widow Toni subsequently became a recluse, spending much of her time watching videos of her former lover as Superman. She had threatened to get even with him, and as things worked out she more than fulfilled that promise. In his will – presumably one he did not have time to change after they broke up – he left her his entire estate, amounting to $71,000.

Was this the action of a man who had suicide in mind? Would he have pulled that trigger, knowing that his fortune would go to his estranged, embittered mistress, and not to the woman he was about to marry, the woman who was now the love of his life?

Ironically that legacy gave the dead actor the last shot. From the grave he reached out to subject his ex-girl friend's husband to a final humiliation. Eddie Mannix could no longer attempt to save face by dismissing his wife's affair as idle gossip. George Reeves's last will and testament made it a matter of public record.

So if Mannix did contrive Superman's shooting, he also shot himself in the foot.

10

THELMA TODD
Mystery of the Laurel and Hardy Blonde

With the weekend behind them, everyone at Hollywood's Roach Studios was ready to resume filming *The Bohemian Girl*, starring Laurel and Hardy. Everyone, that is, except the leading lady. Where was Thelma?

It was Thelma Todd's maid who later that morning of Monday, December 16th, 1935, discovered the answer.

With 70 films to her credit the 30-year-old actress had put her money – plus a loan from her fellow-star Za Su Pitts – into establishing her own café, Thelma Todd's Roadside Rest, on the Pacific Highway between Santa Monica and Malibu.

She lived over the premises, in an apartment with a sliding door connecting it with the apartment of her lover and partner in the venture. This was 48-year-old film director Roland West, who also owned a bungalow with a double garage just 270 steps away up an adjacent hill.

Arriving for work, Thelma's maid wondered where her mistress could be. She was nowhere to be seen in the apartment. The maid looked out of the rear window at West's bungalow on the hill where Thelma kept her car in the garage. The garage doors were ajar, and the maid thought Thelma was probably up there with West.

At 10.30 a.m. she climbed the steps to the bungalow and went into the garage. Thelma's Packard convertible was there and Thelma was slumped in the front seat. The ignition was switched on and the car had idled so long that it ran out of fuel. In the process its exhaust fumes filled the garage, asphyxiating the film star at the wheel.

Her face, evening-gown and mink coat were blood-spattered. There was also blood on the car's seat and running-board, and police called to the scene were in no doubt that they were looking at the victim of a murder.

But then a police spokesman announced that investigators believed Thelma simply lost the key to her apartment, climbed the stairs behind the restaurant and started her car to keep warm. She then either nodded off with the engine running or lost consciousness because of the amount she had drunk.

Thelma's lawyer and her friends thought it was murder, but a blanket of silence was imposed by Hollywood's studio bosses and the inquest jury returned what amounted to an open verdict: "death due to carbon monoxide poisoning."

No one could argue with that, but it still left many questions unanswered. The jurors believed that Thelma's death was accidental. Returning home drunk from a party, she was dropped off by her chauffeur, but later decided to go for a drive.

In her intoxicated state she had started her car, but had neglected to open the garage doors. She had no open wounds, and it was speculated that the blood came from her nose when she slumped on to the steering wheel, also knocking out a false tooth.

This satisfied both the Hollywood establishment and Thelma's mother. It didn't satisfy Thelma's friends or her lawyer. It also conflicted with other evidence.

Hollywood was notorious for its cover-ups. The bigger the star involved in matters best swept under the carpet, the greater was the potential for scandal. And Thelma Todd was big. An ex-teacher and the daughter of a well-known politician, she was talent-spotted after she won a beauty contest and the title Miss Massachusetts. This brought her a place in Paramount's acting school, from which she graduated not just with honours but also with contracts.

Starting with bit-parts, she played opposite Gary Cooper in *Nevada*, and went on to appear with Bing Crosby in *Two for Tonight*. She became Hollywood's most celebrated comedy actress, working with Buster Keaton, Joe E. Brown, and with the Marx Brothers in *Horse Feathers* and *Monkey Business*. But it was her success in short films with Laurel and Hardy that made her a household name.

You can't place her? In Laurel and Hardy's first talkie, *Unaccustomed As We Are* (1929), a beautiful blonde rushes into Stan and Ollie's neighbouring flat after Stan tries to light the gas and there's an explosion. In the ensuing confusion the girl's dress catches fire and Stan and Ollie begin tearing off her clothes. Then her husband and Mrs. Hardy arrive, and Stan and Ollie stuff the half-naked blonde into a trunk...

The beautiful blonde was Thelma, in one of the numerous roles which every film buff will remember. While many stars of silent movies failed to make the transition to talkies, Thelma not only had the right looks but also the right voice. She went on to make a fortune as Hollywood's "Ice Cream Blonde."

Her love-life, though, wasn't nearly as successful as her professional life. Divorced from Pasquale "Pat" DiCicco, a Hollywood talent agent, she subsequently had countless affairs. And although ostensibly still linked to her business-partner Roland West, she was now ditching him as a lover in favour of an unidentified San Francisco businessman she had spoken about to friends.

On the evening of Saturday, December 14th, 1935, she was a guest of honour at a party thrown by the comedian Stanley Lupino and his daughter Ida. The setting was Hollywood's swish Trocadero nightclub, and guests also included Thelma's ex-husband, who she divorced for incompatability and cruelty.

As the two were nevertheless believed to be still on good terms, a place was reserved for DiCiccio next to Thelma. But he arrived with two pretty starlets in tow, snubbing his ex-wife by sitting with them at another table.

Thelma was "very indignant," Ida Lupino recalled. "She berated him bitterly for slighting me and herself." The two had "a terrific argument," according to another guest.

Thelma drank more than was good for her, finally departing in the early hours of Sunday morning in the chauffeur-driven limousine rented for her by her studio.

Ernest Peters was the man at the wheel, and he was to recall that she urged him to drive faster, saying she thought they were being followed by gangsters. Meanwhile Roland West, in his apartment over the café, was phoned by a friend at the party. The friend said that Thelma was on her way home somewhat "under the influence," and he suggested that West should see her safely to bed.

Arriving at the café at 2 a.m., Thelma told her driver to go home. "Don't you want me to walk you up to your apartment?" he asked her, for that was what he usually did.

"That won't be necessary," she replied, and he left.

According to the authorities, he was the last person known to have seen Thelma alive. She subsequently climbed the steps up the hill to West's bungalow, started her car in the garage and perished from the fumes in the early hours of Sunday morning.

Others, however, claimed they had seen Thelma around long after that time. She phoned one witness at 4 p.m., and a chemist said that a woman answering her description used the pay-phone at his drugstore at 11 p.m. that Sunday. Furthermore, the post-mortem found food in her stomach which was eaten just a few hours before her body was discovered at about 10.30 on the Monday morning.

Mrs. Wallace Ford was holding a cocktail party on the Sunday night, and she said that Thelma phoned her at four o'clock to say she would be there, adding: "And when you see who's coming with me, you'll drop dead!"

Whoever that mysterious companion was to be, he never

came forward after Thelma's death.

The actress Jewel Carmen, the estranged wife of Roland West, said she saw Thelma driving through Hollywood after the sun was up on the Sunday morning. Sitting beside Thelma was a good-looking man the witness had never seen before.

Jewel Carmen's account raised other questions. It seemed odd that she should go out of her way to give evidence which favoured the husband who dumped her for Thelma, and who was now considered by many to be an obvious suspect if it were found that the film star was murdered.

As Roland West was in turn jettisoned by Thelma for a San Francisco lover, he certainly had a murder motive, and he was said to be enraged at the way Thelma dropped him for someone who was presumably younger.

Could it be that Jewel was trying to win back her husband's affection with testimony calculated to get him off the hook? Maybe. But West was not being investigated.

At the inquest witnesses were to testify that after Thelma arrived home early on the Sunday morning they heard her screaming obscenities and kicking the door of her apartment.

West said that far from helping Thelma to bed he bolted her door and that of his own apartment against her. He admitted they had a furious row, and an examination of her door supported the accounts that it had been kicked.

West added that shortly after he heard his dog bark at about 3.30 a.m., he heard water running in Thelma's apartment. He assumed that she had somehow managed to gain entry, although her door was still bolted within.

Those who believed he was the killer came up with a novel theory. They speculated that West hired a down-on-her-luck girl to wear Thelma's clothes and scream and kick her door for all to see and hear, while behind that door he knocked Thelma unconscious.

Then, according to the theory, he carried her up the 270 steps to her car, where he dumped her behind the steering-wheel, started the engine and left it running as he departed, leaving the garage doors just ajar. He employed the Thelma look-alike, it was claimed, to give himself an alibi.

Others contended that Thelma's death was suicide. Upset by the earlier events of that night and locked out of her apartment, she went to her car to put an end to her life. District Attorney George Johnson said that remarks she made in recent months indicated depression. He believed she killed herself, for, he said, "it seems too difficult to believe that Miss Todd went to the garage and started the motor of her own car just to keep warm."

The former teacher was regarded as one of the most intelligent actresses around. Even drunk, would she be so stupid as to start her car in a closed garage unless she intended to end her life?

Many of her friends refused to accept the suicide theory. They claimed that Thelma wasn't the suicidal type, and she had everything to live for. Besides, there was no suicide note, and if she really wanted to kill herself she had pills a-plenty – there was no need for her to climb 270 steps.

When Thelma Todd was laid to rest at Forest Lawn cemetery, hundreds assembled to view the open coffin in which she lay surrounded by yellow roses. Za Su Pitts noted how life-like she still appeared. "Why," she said, "she looked as if she were going to sit up and talk!"

What would Thelma have said? Her lawyer thought he knew the answer to that. He disclosed that she had been approached by the notorious entrepreneur of illegal gambling, "Lucky" Luciano, who wanted to use her café as a front for a secret casino upstairs. Her role would be to escort her wealthy patrons to the first floor to try their luck at the tables, a service for which she would be generously rewarded.

Thelma showed Luciano the door, but he was not the sort of man to allow anyone to cross him and get away with it. Moreover, he was not one to reveal his hand to anyone unless he was sure they would remain silent. He was left with no such confidence in Thelma, who in turning him down may have signed her own death warrant.

This was the scenario mapped out by Thelma's lawyer. Claiming he could prove that Luciano was behind Thelma's death, he pressed for a second inquest. This was nervously opposed by Hal Roach, Thelma's studio boss. Like many another member of the Hollywood establishment, he feared Luciano and his henchmen – and not without reason.

Roach talked the district attorney out of agreeing to a second inquest, and Hollywood breathed again. Luciano was not a man to tangle with, and besides, who could tell what might come out at a further inquiry? "Lucky" Luciano could embarrass a lot of people in high places...

Years later Clark Gable was to tell David Niven that Thelma Todd was killed by gangsters, so who can say her lawyer was wrong?

The theory that she was put in her car while unconscious was supported by the fact that she was found still wearing delicate slippers which would have been scuffed if she had climbed all those steps. There wasn't a mark on them.

A further mystery was raised by the post-mortem examination's discovery that Thelma's throat had internal bruising, as if someone had thrust a small bottle down it.

After Roland West and "Lucky" Luciano, her ex-husband was a third suspect. It was claimed that DiCicco not only had a bitter row with Thelma at that party shortly before her death – he was also said to want her back, and to be outraged by the great number of Thelma's lovers who succeeded him.

Roland West, "Lucky" Luciano, "Pat" DiCicco... take your pick. Each was said to have a motive, but for many who knew Thelma, West was the hot favourite. In addition to having a reason for revenge, he was said to be obsessed with the idea of committing the perfect crime.

Among the films he directed were murder mysteries like *Alibi*, *The Bat Whispers*, and *The Monster*. Although the police didn't rate him as a serious suspect, and they never interrogated him in any depth, the mud stuck and Thelma's death finished his career. Cold-shouldered by Hollywood, he never worked again, and he died in obscurity in 1952.

Although Thelma was dead, some felt that she wouldn't lie down. On the morning her body was found, the post brought Stan Laurel and his wife a Christmas card from her, and her Christmas gifts to her friends continued to arrive by mail throughout the rest of the week.

And from beyond the grave she let her ex-husband know precisely what she thought of him. When her will was read a month after her death it was found she had left everything to her mother – except for one derisory dollar bequeathed to "Pat" DiCicco.

Filmgoers were uncomfortably reminded of Thelma's end every time *Monkey Business* was screened. They saw Groucho Marx take her by the arm, telling her: "Now be a good girlie, or I'll lock you up in the garage."

The authorities hadn't heard the last of Thelma, either. One day, the Los Angeles police department received a telegram from Ogden, Utah, signed by a woman who said she had evidence incriminating Thelma Todd's killer. He was living in Ogden, she claimed, where he had taken up residence after the death of the actress.

The police in Ogden were informed. They spoke to the woman, reported to be middle-aged and well-dressed, and reported back to the Los Angeles authorities that the man cited had been found and could be made available for questioning.

So what did the L.A. police do? They didn't put their detectives on the next train. They never followed up the Ogden report, but merely replied to the town's mayor and police department that Thelma's death was considered accidental, and that the case was therefore closed.

11

MAHATMA GANDHI
Violent End for a Man of Peace

Theologians and philosophers have frequently pointed out that Mahatma Gandhi adopted the same tactics as Jesus Christ to achieve his ends. Gandhi's method of dealing with the occupying power was passive resistance, as was Christ's. Both men died for their cause, and by their deaths their causes succeeded.

Gandhi's full name was Mohandas Karamchand Gandhi. His millions of devout followers, who revered him as a saint, called him the Mahatma, the Great Soul. The title was first bestowed on the great Hindu poet Rabindranath Tagore.

Several close observers of Gandhi's life believed that he actually based his day-to-day mode of living on that of Christ, while remaining intrinsically a devout Hindu, with a personal mission to bring understanding to the various factions among the Indian people. For that mission he was assassinated.

The Mahatma was a saintly man by any philosophical standard, opposed to all forms and manifestations of violence, who gave the world a new and effective understanding of the moral power of passive resistance. He was also a man who refused to make enemies, for he cherished the human race.

Although Gandhi was married, according to his people's custom, at the age of 13, he grew up with a firm belief that India's traditional childhood marriages were harmful to the country's progress and against the best interests of simple Hindu folk as a whole. Equally, he was distressed by religious intolerance and the various forms it took.

For countless centuries a crude, cruel and very bloody violence was an integral part of Hindu life. The violent elements had enriched the English language with such meaningful words as "dacoit" and "thug." Submissive violence even permeated marriage contracts. Sutteeism, whereby a widow was obliged to throw herself on her dead husband's funeral pyre, burning herself to death, was one of the most appalling religious rites condoned by a complacent priesthood in any country considering itself civilised.

Gandhi's abhorrence of violence was directed against all the traditional savageness of an intricate caste society. To give full meaning to this side of his character, he stooped to lift the lowly and the downtrodden. When he could not raise them, he joined them in their wretchedness and squalor.

He made it his practice when visiting Delhi to stay in the Sweepers' Colony. The sweepers were among the lowliest of Hindus and when Gandhi made himself one of them it was in furtherance of his belief that a man "has to reduce himself to zero before God will guide him." It was the bedrock of his belief that "God will rule the lives of all those who surrender themselves to Him."

Gandhi's influence in India spanned the years between the two world wars but reached its apogee between the end of the Second World War and the granting of independence to India in 1947. Until independence and the partition which followed it, India's population was predominantly Hindu and Moslem. The two religions were divided into warring factions bitterly and relentlessly opposed to each other.

During the riots the two sides caused, Gandhi made it a point of personal honour to journey to the trouble spots where atrocities committed in the name of religion had occurred. His weapon was the fast – if he could not pacify the warring factions he announced that he would not eat until they settled their differences. And because he was revered by the entire population, it worked.

He remained fasting in the very centre of racial antagonism, suffering physical and mental anguish in silence, a truly pathetic sight to stir men's hearts and affect their consciences, a symbol of something humanly greater than their differences.

Gandhi mutely appealed to their lost respect for humanity. And when it was recovered, he remained with them to ensure that they adhered to the paths of reason and common sense.

In giving himself to poverty and fasting and sustained prayer, he hoped by his example to make his fellows understand that the triumphs of the spirit are greater and more lasting than the victories of vengeance and materialistic self-seeking.

Gandhi was born on October 2nd, 1869. Although his father was a state prime minister, the family's money-lending caste meant that they were not held in high esteem.

When he was 19 he went to London to study law and was called to the Bar by the Inner Temple. Already his fellow-students were prophesying a brilliant future for him, for he dealt in simplicities and had an uncanny ability to go straight to the core of a problem. In 1893 he went to South Africa, where Indian immigrants were subject to oppression, and there for the first time he put into practice his passive resistance principles.

Oriental philosophy had taught him that the strength of Nature lay in her steady persistence along one course of action – or inaction - so he taught his followers that they could most readily achieve their purpose by unitedly refusing co-operation rather than by violence.

As a result, in South Africa his fellow-countrymen achieved their first success over the authorities. Returning to India after the First World War, he began an intensive struggle for Indian independence that brought him into constant conflict with the British authorities. A general boycott of British goods between 1920 and 1922 with accompanying disturbances led to him being sentenced, albeit reluctantly, to six years' imprisonment. Released in 1924, he became president of the Indian National Congress Party.

Gandhi lived simply, largely on goat's milk and vegetables. He hated mechanisation and wove his own loin-cloths, which were often his only garments, urging his followers to follow suit. By 1930 he had such power over the Indian masses that a call to civil disobedience was instantly answered. He was again imprisoned, eventually agreeing with the Viceroy to end such disturbances.

During his many periods of detention he resorted to fasting as a means of forcing the authorities to release him. His great efforts to secure for the lowest caste, the Untouchables, equal status with other castes were directed as much against his own countrymen's prejudices as against the British rulers, who did not want to offend Indian susceptibilities.

Despite his tremendous popularity, he was well aware of the risks he ran. For years he calmly considered the possibility of his own death from violence. He even undertook what he called fasts unto death – as in 1932, when he was championing the cause of the Untouchables.

The Untouchables were India's lowest of the low – denied any form of what we would today call basic human rights. Flying in the face of centuries of convention, Gandhi now described them as children of God, and named his weekly news-sheet *Harijans* after them.

He insisted that they should be accepted into the general community of Hindus and allowed free access to the sacred temples. Sceptics cynically called this particular fast unto death a political stunt, but the Mahatma had an answer for them.

"Fasting stirs up sluggish consciences and fires loving hearts into action," he said. "Those who have to bring about radical changes in human conditions and surroundings cannot do so except by raising ferment in society. There are two methods of doing this – by violence or non-violence. Non-violent pressure exerted through self-suffering by fasting touches and strengthens the moral fibre of those against whom it is directed."

Not everyone liked the sound of that. They saw the Mahatma as an enemy, and his example as a protest to which they had no effective answer, except by continuing the violence Gandhi abhorred. From time to time they conferred among themselves and decided that it would be better for them if Gandhi were out of the way.

But who could remove such a revered and saintly man, except at the certain cost of his own life?

One of the disgruntled was Nathuram Vinayak Godse, a Hindu from Poona who was deeply opposed to racial tolerance throughout the Indian sub-continent. He was 39, and a high-caste member of the Hindu Mahasabha party, which had a long history of violent extremism. He was a man who lived every hour with his obsessions, for he was editor of the intractable Hindu *Mahasabha* weekly newspaper.

Like many an Indian of his time, Godse was fettered by the beliefs with which he had been shackled since early childhood. He grew up to become naturally and tragically a fanatic, unable to see any other viewpoint except his own. In his early years of striving against the British Raj, he had learned the meaning of objective hate.

Gandhi, too, had striven against the British Raj. Like Godse, he wanted an end to British rule in India. But in his case it was without hate. He was stimulated and sustained by a sense of high purpose, perhaps even of destiny.

He was also deeply aware that when independence came (at the outbreak of the Second World War it was left in abeyance until the end of hostilities) there might not be immediate liberty and justice for all. He knew that in the two centuries of British rule the occupying power had presided over vast changes and adaptations of customs and creeds inherited from an alien civilisation - and some of those changes and adaptations were still too new to be entrenched.

The two men, Gandhi and Godse, were poles apart in temperament and outlook. Both came from the wealthy strata of the socially striated Hindu community. Both passionately wanted, and worked for, Indian independence. Both were capable of relentlessly pursuing their goal – the one by violence, the other by non-violence.

Yet the clash of wills that ended in Gandhi's assassination and Godse's execution did not occur, ironically, until after India's independence as a separate nation was established.

When independence was finally achieved, and Lord Mountbatten, the last British Viceroy of India, watched the Union Jack slowly lowered for the last time in 1947, many Indians thought they were about to see a changed and much more joyous way of life. They were soon disillusioned.

The Congress Party fought the elections of that memorable year with a slogan of independence for a united India. That slogan was a sham. Independence was achieved – but there was to be no union.

Almost at once renewed strife and bitterness broke out between the factions. Independence simply seemed to cement ancient rivalries and create a new power structure, plus the inevitable desire among the power-seekers to share in the wealth that power could bring.

The result was the dividing of India permanently and aggressively into two nations, Hindu and Moslem. The two names written on the redrawn map after the hand-over from the British were India and Pakistan. This was harsh political surgery, and the country was butchered and bled from it.

Moslems had striven for a large, powerful Pakistan, but they had to accept an irritating compromise – a restricted homeland, with the partition of the Punjab and of Bengal. The determined Sikhs had demanded a united home country, without Moslem domination. They were presented with a division that cut the Sikhs in two and a Pakistan where the Moslems would be in the threatening ascendant.

This was a deal to breed violence and it duly broke out, both in Bengal and the Punjab. Gandhi hurried to Bengal and quickly quelled the disorders before they got really out of hand. In the Punjab, however, it was a different story.

Homes were burned and looted there, men, women and children were murdered. Communities were plundered and uprooted, and the homeless were sent staggering away in a crazy pattern of enforced migration. As a result, human progress in some of the more violent districts was set back hundreds of years.

Even in Bengal the truce brought about by the presence of the Mahatma was felt to be only temporary. The volcano rumbled. It would be only a matter of time before it erupted.

The pessimists seemed to be proved right when in September of the year of independence terrible rioting broke out. In Calcutta hundreds were murdered, Moslem corpses cluttered the bazaars and back alleys.

Gandhi, a bowed old man of 78, whose physical resistance to demands put upon his spare frame by his uncompromising attitude to the trouble-makers was weakening considerably as the months passed, announced another fast until death.

He would, this time, fast, and continue fasting, until the communal slaughter on the streets of Calcutta stopped. Only when blood ceased to flow would he break this reproachful fast. With India in turmoil, it was undoubtedly to be the bravest act of his life.

The announcement of the new fast unto death was received by millions in Calcutta with a sense of shamed shock that plunged through the entire community. The picture of the little old man sitting in a corner, his bony frame bowed in meditation and prayer for their erring ways, had the same effect as a stunning physical blow upon them. And within hours the senseless slaughter ceased.

Almost a quarter of Calcutta's teeming population was Moslem. Their leading newspaper said of Gandhi as he ended his fast: "He was ready to die, so that we might live peacefully."

So the man of peace had performed a modern miracle. But in so doing he had ensured his own eventual death by violence.

On January 13th, 1948, the sight of a divided country now haggling bitterly over Kashmir, left, in his own phrase, "nothing but agony" in his heart. That agony was to be the signal for yet another fast unto death. It was to be his last.

He had announced his intention the previous day, when he proclaimed publicly: "I have no answer for the Moslem friends who see me from day to day about what they should do. My impotence has been gnawing at me of late. It will go immediately the fast is undertaken. I have been brooding over it for the past three days. The final conclusion has flashed upon me and makes me happy.

"No man, if he is pure, has anything more precious to give than his life. I hope and pray that I have the purity in me to justify this step."

The fast lasted five tremulous days – until January 18th, when the Mahatma was told that as a result a peace committee representing all the various communities in Delhi had met and signed a pact of friendship. The pact stipulated that the signatories agreed to protect the life, property and faith of the Moslem minority.

The man of peace had performed yet another miracle, and all India breathed a deep sigh of heartfelt gratitude to him. But some of the truth was hidden.

Even while Gandhi was fasting, there were fanatics who eyed him and his purpose as inimical to their interests and considered that he must now be destroyed. Among them was Gandhi's implacable high-caste enemy, Nathuram Godse, who had watched the granting of independence with a sense of triumph. But Godse had already made up his mind that he could not live in the same world as

Mahatma Gandhi. The zero quality to which Gandhi reduced himself in the social scale was a lasting reproach to this man of iron-hard prejudice who would not tolerate any compromise in his beliefs.

At a secret meeting the anti-Gandhi conspirators decided to hire a gullible youth to assassinate their enemy. The plan was nothing if not crude – the youth, Madan Lal, a Punjabi refugee, was expected to kill the Mahatma by hurling a bomb at him.

Gandhi had moved out of Sweepers' Colony and was now much more comfortable settled in Birla House, in Albuquerque Road, New Delhi. This was the home of G. D. Birla, a wealthy Hindu industrialist who admired and adored the little old wrinkled man who performed miracles through his faith and poverty.

Birla House was set in a large garden, through whose gates streamed people anxious to see the Mahatma and listen to his words. Some even came simply to touch him. Gandhi held regular prayer meetings for them – his own special kind of social gatherings for purging the heart.

On January 20th, two days after he had broken what was to be his last fast, the crowd collected for the Mahatma's customary prayer meeting. In the silence, broken only by his soft voice, there was a sudden sharp bomb explosion, followed by cries of fear and alarm and anger.

The crowd, excited and outraged, seized Madan Lal, who had been seen to throw the bomb into the compound and was being held by an old woman of remarkable courage.

But Lal did not have the necessary temperament for a successful assassin, especially in violent India. His bomb exploded without doing any real damage, and amazingly no one in the large crowd was hurt. Its message, though, was not lost on Gandhi.

He was aware of the enemies for whom his would-be assassin was working. They were the power-hungry who preferred death to reasoned argument. Death was an attractive short-cut that got results in a hurry.

He had heard them whispering during his last fast: "Let Gandhi die. He should have died on Independence Day." At that point the Mahatma knew that he was marked down for death.

He did not allow the warning to change his way of life. His sole concern after the bomb-throwing incident was for the future of Madan Lal. He told his followers that more mature minds had filled the youth with hate. Thus, to a police official after the arrest, Gandhi said: "I do not want him to be harassed."

The police official bowed respectfully but said nothing. He had a job to do, there were rules to be obeyed. Gandhi sighed and said: "I would prefer that you try to win him to a right way of thinking and behaving."

Then the Mahatma addressed the crowd who had come to the prayer meeting. He said: "I expect you all to continue praying, in spite of exploding bombs or showering bullets." This was his simple answer to the believers in violence.

His calm after the Birla House incident appeared to many of his followers to be unnatural. What was most likely in his mind was an awareness that he still had to keep an appointment with violence that would result in his own death. His premonition was to be correct.

Six days after the bomb-throwing, on January 26th, Gandhi prepared for one of his customary busy days. His followers noted that there were few signs of a celebrant about the Mahatma that morning, or at a meeting he held later that day in the grounds of Birla House.

He was heard to say to those close to him: "Now that we have independence, we all seem to be rather disillusioned. At least, I am, even if you are not."

The Mahatma was not in the habit of speaking so frankly. It was as if he himself had announced that his time had come.

Four days later, on Friday, January 30th, Gandhi was still pondering the fate of Madan Lal, aware that those who had inspired the lad would continue to make attempts on his life until he was killed. The Mahatma had slept badly that night and rose early. He was immediately joined by his faithful attendant, Bishwan.

"Bring me all my important letters," Gandhi said, in a voice which Bishwan remembered was "rather dreamy," as though his thoughts were far away. "I must reply to them today, for tomorrow I may never be."

The words were extraordinarily prophetic, for this was to be the Mahatma's last day on Earth.

The subtle, formal atmosphere continued through the day until 4 p.m., when India's Deputy Prime Minister, Sardar Vallabhbhai Patel, arrived at Birla House.

Gandhi advised his visitor that it would be in India's interest if Patel and the Prime Minister, Pandit Nehru, were to work more closely together, which wasn't happening at the moment. He told Patel that each of the two ministers was dependent on the goodwill of the other, particularly because some members of the Indian Congress were out to destroy the unity of the governing Congress Party.

Gandhi, now nearly 80, and aware that he might be murdered at any moment, said to Patel: "I have written to Mr. Nehru upon this same matter and told him, my friend, what I am telling you."

The two men talked for more than an hour. It was five minutes past five when Gandhi realised that he was already late for the expectant crowd outside. He took his leave of Patel and, helped by his two cousins, Abha and Manu, on whose arms he leaned his fragile frame, he started for the prayer meeting.

He left the house by the back entrance and moved towards the lawn in front of an open stonework pavilion. The crowd was a dozen deep on each side of a green aisle, along which the Mahatma made his slow way to the low table covered with a fresh white cloth, standing in front of the stone pavilion. On the cloth lay his white prayer cushion.

The crowd hushed and pressed about. Among them was

Gandhi's sworn enemy, Nathuram Godse, wearing a khaki jacket. He had come to Delhi after learning that the exploding bomb tossed by fellow-conspirator Madan Lal had failed to kill the Mahatma.

Godse's fanatical eyes glared at Gandhi. He pushed his hand into his khaki jacket and his fingers closed around the butt of a Beretta .38 automatic pistol.

The tottering Mahatma, supported by his two smiling cousins, was walking very slowly and with great difficulty, one foot pushing feebly in front of the other. When he was only a few feet away, Godse brought his hands together as a Hindu does when he is about to pray, making the *namaskar* – a sign of obeisance.

Prayer, though, was far from his thoughts. Merely standing there in the mixed crowd of Gandhi worshippers, some of whom genuinely believed the Mahatma was the incarnation of God, made Godse furious to the limits of his high-caste soul. Even so, his face managed a smile intended to register both humility and gratitude as he raised his pressed-together hands before his face and bowed stiffly from the waist.

Gandhi glanced at this smooth-faced stranger with the round features, hooked nose and close-cropped hair. As the Mahatma looked away Godse's hand slid back into his pocket holding the Beretta. He drew the pistol and swung it round in an arc. He fired three times at close range, and the three bullets tore into the Mahatma's frail body.

"Ram! Ram!" – "Oh, God! Oh, God!" cried the stricken Mahatma. The first bullet had entered his stomach, the second and third rocked him backwards, jerking his head with pain and shock. His thin-framed spectacles became unhooked from one ear and dangled grotesquely across his brown, wrinkled face. He stumbled, his loose-fitting sandals falling from his thin feet.

Blood welled and gushed from his perforated stomach and chest. His hands slid from the shoulders of his two cousins trying desperately to keep him upright. Tears welled in the eyes of Manu and she gave a thin cry of shocked despair.

Gandhi's fragile, shaking hands fluttered in a gesture of prayer, while the stunned audience gazed first at his crumpled body and then at Godse with the smoking gun and the smoky hot eyes.

A sudden wailing rose from the crowd. Godse was seized as Gandhi was borne by friends and relatives to Birla House. The white-covered table and the white prayer cushion looked suddenly forlorn as the lawns emptied, revealing bright beads of fresh blood shining like rubies on the grass.

The Mahatma lost consciousness before he was carried into Birla House. He was taken into a ground-floor room, placed gently on the floor and covered with a sheet from feet to chin.

Relatives and friends knelt all around him, some of them intoning scriptural verses. One of those at his side was Deputy Prime Minister Patel, who only minutes before had been speaking to the Mahatma about the future of the country and the difficulties facing the new government. There Gandhi's life rapidly ebbed away. For a moment or two the only sound in the death room was the wailing of the crowd, carried through the open window like a lament.

His prophetic awareness of his approaching end had turned out to be all too true, and his last conscious words were a call to the God he had served with a devotion equalled by few men.

The news spread though New Delhi with the speed of a monsoon. Thousands poured into Birla House, wailing and wringing their hands. The shocked Prime Minister, Pandit Nehru, addressed the nation over the radio.

In a choked voice he said: "The light has gone out of our lives, and there is darkness everywhere." He paused, then added: "The father of the nation is no more." His voice grew stronger, as if he were making a determined effort to control his emotion. "The best prayer we can offer him and his memory is to dedicate ourselves to truth and to the cause for which this great countryman of ours lived – and for which he died."

Gandhi's body lay in state at Birla House, where his relatives placed flower petals on his face and around his thin, hunger-wasted body, now draped in white homespun cloth.

Next day a flower-decked army vehicle arrived to carry the Mahatma's remains to the banks of the River Jumna. Crowds lined the five-mile route and along every yard of the way bright petals fell. Behind the hearse, where Pandit Nehru sat alongside Gandhi's body, the mourners stretched for miles.

There were flowers everywhere, for every embassy and consulate in New Delhi had sent a floral tribute. Lord Mountbatten, the former viceroy, was there to salute the carriage, which was drawn by representatives of the new nation's army, navy and air force. The incredible procession was accompanied by the mournful sounds of trumpets and large conches.

Hundreds of thousands were waiting when the cortege reached Raj Hjat, on the banks of the Jumna. Indian Air Force Dakotas swept down from the sky, releasing thousands of petals across the bier. Pandit Nehru, deeply affected by the occasion, walked to the dead Mahatma's feet, bent down and kissed them reverently.

The Prime Minister remained standing at the foot of the funeral pyre. At its head stood the Mahatma's son, Devadas. A flame touched the pyre and there was a swift and lurid flare. Sandalwood, camphor and incense were thrown on to the flames. A pall of smoke rose and drifted before a steady breeze.

Gandhi's ashes were taken to Allahbad to be immersed in three sacred rivers – the Saraswati, the Ganges and the Jumna. Another multitude gathered for the ceremony, standing along the river banks chanting hymns. Thousands of them swam into the confluence of the rivers while aircraft showered flowers on the urn carried in a slowly-drifting boat.

When the handful of powdery ashes were immersed in

the waters, all that remained of Mahatma Gandhi was the memory of the man of peace – and the nation he had fathered.

On May 26th, 1948, nine conspirators stood trial for their part in a series of events that ended with the assassination in the grounds of Birla House. The trial did not end until November 30th, and formal sentence was not delivered until the following year, on February 10th.

Nathuram Godse and a supporter who had actively abetted him, Narain Apte, were sentenced to be hanged. Many followers of Gandhi protested at this, pointing out that such violent retribution was against everything that the Mahatma had stood for. But the sentence was eventually carried out.

At the trial Godse told the court: "I sat brooding on the atrocities perpetrated on Hinduism and its dark and deadly future if left to face Islam outside and Gandhi inside. All of a sudden, I decided to take the extreme step against Gandhi. Before I fired the shots I actually wished him well and bowed to him in reverence."

Madan Lal, whose bomb attempt on the Mahatma's life was bungled, and four other conspirators, were sent to prison for life. One of the defendants was acquitted. Another earned a Judas freedom by betraying his fellow-conspirators and turning State's evidence.

The men who had wanted Gandhi dead did not make a brave show when the hour of reckoning arrived for them. Possibly they were depressed at having earned the contempt and loathing of so many millions of their fellow-countrymen. They themselves had so far to travel to reach that human zero achieved by the man they plotted to destroy.

12

SUNNY VON BULOW
Tons of Money, Tons of Pills

Few women in America suffered from the new disease of affluenza quite as badly as did Sunny von Bulow. Affluenza afflicts the incredibly rich: the disease comes about because they have so much money they don't know what to do with themselves, and so they become sick of life.

Sunny and her husband Claus von Bulow devoted all their energies and all their waking hours to maintaining the social graces of the idle rich. That, of course, can be incredibly boring, and can lead to the disease with which most of us are unfamiliar.

When the couple made up their minds to become permanent fixtures of Rhode Island society they looked for the finest mansions up for sale in the swank resort of Newport. They settled on Clarendon Court – the ivy-covered palace made famous in the 1950s when the movie *High Society* was filmed there.

Although Claus was a British lawyer by profession and a former right-hand man to oil baron J. Paul Getty, he did not work during the years in Newport. Sunny, who was by far the richer of the two, preferred to have him around all the time.

Both were striking figures. Claus, 6ft. 4in tall, was massively built, ebullient and extrovert. Sunny, tall, slim, beautiful, was despite her background incredibly shy and introverted. They were a couple who caused heads to turn not just for their wealth but for their looks.

Together they devoted themselves to throwing the most elaborate formal parties in Newport since the billionaire colony's golden era, which was way back in the 1900s. When they weren't partying they spent a considerable amount of time commuting between their other homes – on Fifth Avenue, New York, and Belgrave Square, London.

Never shy of publicity, theirs was a life-style that made them the darlings of the gossip columns. Their summer parties, held about four times a year, were semi-intimate affairs, with no more than 60 guests and just a few extra servants. They were held on the terrace next to the illuminated reflecting pools surrounded by gushing fountains. Music was supplied by the Cliff Hall Orchestra, the favourite of Newport society.

When Sunny and Claus wanted to throw a real shindig, like the one they hosted in the summer of 1980 for the 21st birthday of Prince Alexander von Auersperg, Sunny's son from her former marriage, it was something special.

Everyone was asked to dress in white, and of course everyone complied. The men wore white suits and boaters, the women gauzy pale dresses that might have come straight out of a Victorian novel. Croquet courts were set up on the vast lawn. It was a party that would never be forgotten – not even by the jaded social lions of Newport, some of whom were themselves feeling the symptoms of affluenza.

Sunny, whose real name was Martha, was one of the wealthiest women in America. She was born into a family of almost unimaginable riches, believed to be linked to the Carnegie fortune. Her father, George Crawford, was the former chairman of the Columbia Gas and Electric Corporation of Pittsburgh. After his death, when she was three years old, Sunny was brought up by her mother and grandmother.

Doted upon by the two women, Sunny blossomed into a

radiant blonde beauty, with a remarkable likeness to another society lioness of that era – Grace Kelly. Although she was a painfully shy young woman, her warm personality was responsible for her nickname.

As a young woman she fell passionately in love with the scion of a princely Russian family that had lost all its money. The young man, who spoke 10 languages, was working as a humble translator, and since his prospects did not appear to extend beyond a translator's modest salary, Sunny's family pressured her into ditching him.

To help her forget the wounds of this first romance, they shipped her off to the posh Austrian ski resort of Schloss Mitterzill, where she met most of the playboys who wintered there. Very soon she was being romantically linked to another prince, Alfie von Auersperg, the Schloss Mitterzill tennis pro, whose family fortune had also disappeared generations ago.

This time the family couldn't keep the lovers apart, and in 1957, when she was 25, Sunny married Prince Alfie. Her great wealth enabled them to live lavishly in Austria and Germany, to spend their summers in Venice and in-between times, to spend a lot of time in Paris and New York.

Sunny bore the prince two children – a daughter named Annie Laurie but called Ala by everyone, and Alexander, who inherited through his father the right to call himself a prince, a form of titular address that mystifies vast numbers of Europeans who believe that the nation states from which such titles spring have been republics for the best part of a century.

Despite the tinselly glamour of new-fashioned wealth and distinctly old-fashioned title, the marriage didn't take. Prince Alfie was fooling around with other women and not trying very hard to hide it from his wife. Sunny began drinking too much and it was clear to their friends that things couldn't go on much longer like this.

And they were right. After eight years of marriage Prince Alfie left Sunny for another woman and went off to hunt in Kenya. Sunny donated him a handsome settlement, went away with the kids, and kept on drinking. Then, one day she phoned Prince Alfie's sister in London, saying she was coming over for a visit. The former sister-in-law got in touch with a friend, who lined up Claus von Bulow as an escort. Sunny had already met Claus several times in New York. But their meetings in London were different. This time she was a single woman, and very soon she was in love again.

Claus von Bulow was Danish. He was born in 1926 into an upper-class family in Denmark – his grandfather, Fritz Bulow, was minister of justice in the Danish government, and his father, Svend Borberg, was a playwright and drama critic for a Copenhagen newspaper.

When Claus was four, his parents divorced and he went to live with his mother. When he was seven he was sent to boarding school in Switzerland. He was there for four years when, in 1940, the Nazis marched into Denmark. Two years after that Claus escaped to England, where his mother was making her home.

The war proved no impediment to Claus's determination to succeed. He was only 16 when he became a Cambridge University undergraduate at Trinity College, and at 21 he had obtained a degree in law. Perhaps because his father had been convicted as a minor Nazi collaborator and served 18 months in prison, he now adopted his mother's maiden name, styling himself Claus von Bulow.

He lived briefly in post-war Paris, studying political science at the Sorbonne, before returning to England. For a while he worked in a London bank, then he entered the chambers of Lord Hailsham, QC, as a barrister practising criminal law.

In 1959, Claus was spotted by J. Paul Getty. The American oil magnate wanted a chief executive assistant and Claus fitted the job like a glove. Claus bought and sold companies for Getty, presided over disputes, set up oil refineries, jetted round the world and looked set to take over the entire Getty oil empire. On one of his trips, in

1960, he ran into Sunny for the first time. They met again at dinner four years later. In 1965 the globe-trotting lawyer began dating the wealthy divorcee on his frequent business trips to New York, where she was living with her children.

On June 6th, 1966, they were married. Claus was 40 years old, Sunny six years his junior. The following year Sunny gave birth to a daughter, named Cosima.

To all appearances, the marriage appeared to be a success. Sunny cut down on her drinking and Claus was a loving dad to all three of her children. But as the years went by Sunny's health began to deteriorate, and she started hitting the bottle again. Only on rare occasions now did she go out. Claus, who did not work, because she demanded that he should always be with her, became a virtual prisoner. Even so, he kept in touch with his friends by spending as much time as Sunny could spare him at New York's exclusive Knickerbocker Club.

Claus confided to his intimates that Sunny had stopped having sex with him not long after their daughter Cosima was born. And as so often happens in parallel circumstances, Claus met and fell in love again. This time the attraction was the daughter of one of his old Danish friends, a dark-haired actress named Alexandra Islas, who appeared to be quite lonely herself in the wake of her recent divorce from a New York banker.

Although friends counselled Claus to leave Sunny, marry his new girl friend and seize what might be his last chance of happiness, he refused. If he left Sunny, he explained, she would undoubtedly try to kill herself – and he would be blamed. Some, however, decided that his motives for staying put were rather less lofty. If he split from his wife, they whispered, he would have to cut back on his sumptuous lifestyle.

Feeling a bit trapped, Claus sought relief in work. Although Sunny resented his taking a job, he invested heavily in the theatre and made a big score when the comedy-thriller *Deathtrap* proved to be a box office hit.

Although he didn't fare nearly as well with his next

investment, a musical called *Carmelina,* he was enjoying his new life as a working man. It involved him among other things with a group of art dealers who ran an art-investment fund, and as a consultant to a New York brokerage firm who paid him a handsome salary.

Claus, in fact, was now all things to all businesses, a role he loved to play. The problem was, the more successful he was in the business world, the more difficult Sunny became.

A few days before Christmas, 1979, she told her daughter Ala that she was thinking of divorcing Claus. She would make an extremely generous provision for her husband, she said, but she was tired of him.

Claus and Sunny spent that Christmas at Clarendon Court in Newport with their family, as they had done on a number of Christmases past. Early in the evening of December 26th Prince Alexander thought that his mother didn't look too well, and took her upstairs to her bedroom. Later the family maid, Maria Schrallhammer, went upstairs to check on Sunny's condition.

"She was lying on her bed," the maid would later recall. "I thought she was fast asleep."

Next morning Claus told Maria that Sunny wasn't feeling well and so she needn't bother with making the bed. Prince Alexander went out to play tennis with a few friends and didn't see his mother, either. That afternoon, though, the maid went into Sunny's room to make sure everything was all right.

"I found Mrs. von Bulow unconscious on the bed," she later recalled. "Mr. von Bulow was lying right next to her. I told him that she was unconscious and that we should call a doctor. He replied, 'No, she's sleeping.' But I tried to wake her up and she was unconscious. I took her hand and said, 'Madame, wake up.' But there was no response.

"Mr. von Bulow insisted that she was only sleeping. He told me that they didn't sleep at all the previous two nights.

"I left the room, but came back later. I found Mrs. von Bulow in the same condition and I asked him again to call the doctor – and her mother. And he told me, 'No, she's sleeping.' And this went on all day long, until the evening."

When Prince Alexander came home from playing tennis around 4.30 that afternoon he would say, "The maid came right up to me and said something was very wrong. I went directly to my mother's room and found her lying on her bed. I shook her, tried to rouse her. She was in a state of unconsciousness...I just recall shaking her and there was no response at all. My stepfather came up to me and asked me, 'What should I do?' I said, 'Call the doctor.' And he did."

As they waited for the doctor to come, Maria decided that she did not like the sound of her mistress's breathing.

"I picked her up," she recalled, "and she just couldn't breathe any more. I was really afraid that she would die before the doctor arrived."

When Dr. Janis Gailitis arrived he found Sunny comatose. Her breathing suddenly stopped and he had to give her artificial respiration to revive her. He called an ambulance knowing that by the time it arrived at Newport Hospital she would be close to death. Her blood-sugar level was so low on admission that hospital doctors fed her glucose intravenously. Then a strange thing happened. Instead of rising, her blood-sugar level fell even more. Before the doctors could take the necessary action, the blood-sugar level began rising, and she regained consciousness.

At this point the doctors around her bedside thought they knew what was happening. They suspected that Sunny was hypoglycaemic – the victim of an ailment in which the blood-sugar level drops so low that dizziness results.

That wasn't the initial view of Sunny's own GP, however. At first he suspected that the cause of her coma was simply alcohol abuse.

"I continued to believe this," he would say, "until several weeks later, when I received the transcript of the report from Newport Hospital, indicating that the blood-alcohol level on admission was zero – that in fact Mrs. von Bulow hadn't taken any alcohol."

The report also showed that a test for barbiturates had proved negative, leaving the doctor undecided about what had caused Sunny's coma.

Sunny recovered and was discharged from hospital several days later. But over the next year, her health deteriorated. On April 21st, 1980, she went into New York City's Columbia-Presbyterian Hospital for tests. Doctors now wanted to determine whether she had a tumour on her pancreas, which would have caused an excess of insulin and would explain her coma.

The tests were negative. The doctors then diagnosed her as "reactive hypoglycaemic," and told her she must abstain from alcohol and sugar from that time on.

More than seven months later, on December 1st, Claus entered the bedroom of the New York hotel where they were staying together and found Sunny unconscious on the floor. She was bleeding from the head. He called for an ambulance, which rushed her to Lenox Hill Hospital. There doctors determined that she was suffering from a salicylate overdose – in simple words, from aspirin poisoning. She was said to take 10 to 20 aspirin tablets every day.

Again Sunny recovered and again she was discharged from hospital. Later that month, on Friday, December 19th, Claus, Sunny and Cosima went up to Newport for a weekend stay at Clarendon Court. Prince Alexander, now a student at Brown University, in nearby Providence, Rhode Island, came along to join them. On Saturday night they all went out together to a movie. When they arrived back home Alexander had a private talk with his mother.

Sunny's speech seemed to him at that moment to be quite slurred. Remembering her coma of the year before, he became worried. Sunny assured him that she was all right, that she hadn't taken any sleeping pills. Nevertheless, her speech became even more incomprehensible and it seemed to her son that she was becoming weaker and weaker before his very eyes. Deeply concerned, he carried her next door to her bedroom, then told his stepfather what had happened.

Sunny did not come down for breakfast next morning. At about 10.30 Claus came in from a walk with the dogs and went to her bedroom to see what was keeping her. Minutes later, he hurried downstairs and asked Alexander to come with him to the bedroom. Sunny was sprawled face-down on the white marble floor.

An ambulance was called to take her back to Newport Hospital within the hour. Once again she had slipped into a hypoglycaemic coma - one from which doctors said she would never emerge. The diagnosis was that at least 60 per cent of her brain was functionally dead.

Even though doctors had diagnosed Sunny as a "reactive hypoglycaemic," meaning that her body would produce too much insulin if she consumed a large amount of sugar – which would then make her blood-sugar level drop precipitously – they were still shocked that she had fallen into such a deep coma.

A coma so deep, in fact, that they concluded that it must have been brought on by an injection of insulin, rather than by internal production.

Under its effects Sunny fell into a sleep from which she could not be wakened. Despite the life support machine to which she was wired up, her brain became a vegetable. She could, it was thought, go on living for years with proper medical care, but she would never recover.

Told of the doctors' findings, Ala and Alexander consulted an aggressive Manhattan lawyer, a former assistant district attorney. The lawyer investigated and took his findings to the DA's office. Although the New York prosecutor had no jurisdiction in the case, he advised the office of the Rhode Island attorney general to investigate.

The attorney general's office did just that, and three months later, in April, 1981, presented its findings to a grand jury in Newport. On Monday, July 6th, the jury returned two indictments charging Claus von Bulow with attempting to murder his wife by means of massive doses of insulin – once on December 27th, 1979, and again on December 21st, 1980.

Daniel Hackett, a spokesman for the attorney general, declared resolutely: "If you have hypoglycaemia and you are given insulin to break it up you are in dire straits. We therefore allege that Claus von Bulow injected his wife with insulin, knowing it could be fatal."

But von Bulow's lawyer swiftly countered with a quite different explanation for Sunny's ill-health. "She had some tremendous psychological problems," he declared. "And there is some evidence that she was suicidal. She has made statements to people that she no longer wanted to live."

On Monday, February 1st, 1982, at the end of a lengthy pre-trial hearing to determine the admissibility of some controversial evidence, the 12 jurors together with four reserve jurors empanelled to hear the case, were taken on a tour of Clarendon Court.

In court the following day the prosecutor, Stephen Famiglietti, alleged that an overdose of insulin which had left Sunny in an irreversible coma was "a clandestine and ingenious attempt by her husband ... to secretly murder her" with a drug which "up until a few years ago was undetectable in the human body."

As the drug took effect, he added, Claus had remained in the house, waiting for her to die.

Claus's counsel, Herald Fahringer, countered by portraying the defendant as a talented gentleman of independent means, a long-suffering husband who had tolerated his wife's illness and refusal to let him work or engage in sexual relations with her.

"If there's one thing we really resent in this case," he told the jury, "it is the innuendo that he was acting in an unhusbandly fashion."

Defence counsel said that Sunny had told her husband after the birth of Cosima that she had lost all interest in sex. He could satisfy his needs however he wished, so long as he was discreet.

Sunny's daily routine, he said, at least during her stays in

New York, consisted of rising at 11 a.m., having breakfast in bed, taking a chauffeured car to "an exclusive women's gym," followed by a visit to the hairdresser's, a shopping expedition and a nap.

Despite her hypoglycaemia, he went on, Sunny ate too many sweets, drank too much, smoked four to five packets of cigarettes a day, consumed 20 aspirins, two dozen laxative pills and a host of tranquillisers, including Seconal, Valium and barbiturates.

He thought she had probably been felled by an overdose of Amobarbitol, and said: "What happened to her was no one's fault but her own."

The prosecution's first witness was Prince Alexander, Sunny's 22-year-old son, who said that late in 1980 his mother told him that she had to get a divorce. "She wasn't happy. I asked her why. She said it was something so horrible that she didn't want to tell me."

His only knowledge of his mother's barbiturate use was what his stepfather had told him, he said. But on three occasions in the time between his mother's two comas he had seen in Claus's wardrobe a "black bag" which contained a number of drugs.

On each occasion Maria Schrallhammer, his mother's maid, had shown him the bag. The second time she removed a short-necked bottle from the bag and asked him: "What is insulin for?" He did not look at the label himself.

Cross-examined, Alexander agreed that he had spent "somewhere in the neighbourhood of $100,000" to look into his mother's illness. It was clear to the court that the defence was trying to convince the jury that Sunny's children's interest in prosecuting their stepfather was purely financial.

Alexander was asked about a conversation in January, 1981, which the children had had with Claus about the possibility of releasing some of the servants at Clarendon Court because of the rising cost of medical expenses.

"Didn't your stepfather indicate to you on that occasion

that you and your sister would each receive about $15 million under the terms of your mother's will?" he was asked.

"Yes, I think he did," Alexander replied.

The prosecution submitted to the court some hypodermic needles, vials of pills, liquids and powders and an empty box of Lidocaine, which Alexander and a private detective, Edwin Lambert, allegedly took from Claus's study and his locked cupboard at Clarendon Court.

The maid, Maria Schrallhammer, said in evidence that Claus had lied to a doctor about his wife's condition as she lay unconscious after her initial coma. She said that Claus phoned a doctor to say that Sunny had got out of bed to go to the bathroom when in fact she had not moved from her bed since morning.

"I left the room because what he said wasn't true," she declared. "I was upset. I didn't tell him because he wouldn't have liked it." Claus, she insisted, had refused to phone a doctor all day, although she had been urging him to do so since 9.30 that morning, when she came into Sunny's bedroom and found her "ice cold."

Two days before Sunny's second coma, she went on, she found a vial of insulin, some hypodermic needles, and a syringe in a small black bag which Claus was bringing to Newport from the Manhattan apartment. She added that in 1969, during a holiday in Majorca, Claus had given himself a couple of vitamin injections.

She disputed Claus's claim that Sunny had granted him carte blanche for extra-marital sex. She claimed that besides keeping a mistress, he also visited a prostitute on a regular basis. Only weeks after the start of Sunny's second coma, she found receipts from a motel in the Bahamas, where Claus spent Valentine's Day with his mistress.

And she denied allegations that Sunny had a drinking problem, or that she gorged herself on sweets and drugs. "She had a glass of alcohol just once in a while," the maid said. "I can see nothing wrong with that."

A Newport Hospital doctor said in evidence that he was

suspicious of the cause of Sunny's coma, because he had heard of some unexplained circumstances surrounding her first coma a year earlier. He had restarted Sunny's heart after she went into cardiac arrest, but was unable to bring her out of the coma.

"Mrs. von Bulow was deeply comatose – the most severe case of coma I've ever seen. She had a temperature of 81.6 degrees – 17 degrees below normal – with no measurable blood pressure or response to pain stimuli. This patient was so critically cold that we needed to reheat her."

The doctor said that Claus von Bulow came into the emergency room "just a few steps behind the rescue squad" and later joined him in a room about 30 yards away. Claus told the doctor that his wife had been in "the usual state of health the night before, with no intake of alcohol."

While the doctor was talking to Claus a nurse ran in to report that Mrs. von Bulow had stopped breathing. He ran back to the patient's side and gave her emergency inhalation treatment. "The breathing then came back as shallow respiration. I did not leave her bedside from then on for a long time."

Although traces of the barbiturate Amobarbitol were found in Sunny's blood and urine when she was brought to the hospital, the doctor thought the amount "was not really that high for a toxic level." But the body did show "an incredibly high insulin level." When considered with her unusually low blood-sugar count, these "do not go together in a normal person."

Shown a hypodermic needle which, it was claimed, was found in the black bag removed from Claus's cupboard in Newport, the doctor identified it as a small needle which, if used correctly, would not leave a mark.

A hushed expectancy fell upon the court when Alexandra Isles, Claus's mistress, was called to give evidence. She admitted she had once given Claus an ultimatum to marry her within a span of time which expired two months before Sunny's second coma.

She had been intimate with Claus, she said, since March, 1979. When Claus was being investigated by the police her lawyer had advised her to stop seeing him.

Of the allegation against him she said, "I thought it was a pack of nonsense." Asked if she still felt the same way, she replied, "I don't know."

She first met von Bulow at a Knickerbocker Club lunch in April, 1978. A year later he broached the subject of marriage. "I was surprised," she said. "But I loved him."

On December 27th, 1980, when she was visiting Ireland, Claus phoned her to say that Sunny had slipped into a coma, brought on by liquor and pills. When she returned to the United States, they began seeing each other twice a week and even went on holiday together with their children, "as an experiment to see if we could live together as a family."

"Do you still love the defendant?" the prosecutor, Mr. Famiglietti, asked her.

"I don't know," she replied.

Dr. George Cahill, of the Harvard Medical School, told the court that both Sunny's comas were the result of hypoglycaemia, brought on by too much insulin. "Only insulin could have been responsible for them," he said.

He was asked about an opening statement to the jury made by one of Claus's lawyers who said that the first coma was brought on because Sunny had consumed a large eggnog.

Dr. Cahill replied: "I can't think of a better antidote for hypoglycaemia."

The next witness was Sunny's banker, who told the court that Claus stood to inherit a tax-free $14 million out of Sunny's $75 million, on her death.

An exercise instructor at Sunny's posh New York gym told the court that in 1978 Sunny had told her that injections of vitamin B or insulin would help her lose weight and also suggested an injection of Valium to calm her down at the end of the day. Although not saying that Sunny had told her she was giving herself injections, she did quote Sunny as saying that it was easy to inject yourself and that someone had taught her how to do it.

A medical expert at Rhode Island Hospital said that although he hadn't treated Sunny, "from the record, the picture emerging is of a woman with potentially serious psychiatric problems, excess use of tranquillisers, aspirin, tobacco and alcohol, a profound metabolic abnormality of hypoglycaemia and a very low body temperature during the episode which has resulted in her present coma."

He added: "Following the birth of her youngest daughter Mrs. von Bulow experienced five or six days of total paralysis – not due to physical, but psychological causes." Since 1967, she had had "the incredible history of taking 24 laxatives a day for 24 years."

A psychiatrist who spoke to Sunny four days after the first coma, testified that she had told him she was "almost never happy" and "often wished herself dead... She said she was frequently bored and didn't like getting up in the morning.

"She said that she and her husband had grown steadily apart, and it was no longer a satisfactory relationship at all. My overall impression was that she was very neurotic and desperately in need of psychiatric help."

In his final argument to the jury, Prosecutor Famiglietti said: "There are a number of questions that will never have answers. A jury can blow away the smoke and fog to grasp the truth and hold on to it."

Mr. Farmiglietti reminded the jury that the von Bulows were considering divorce in the months before Sunny's coma. "This made his motive even stronger, for while she was considering divorce she could have changed her will at any time.

"He had grown accustomed to a style of life which he was not willing to give up. With her death, he could have lived lavishly, splendidly, with the woman he loved."

But Mr. Fahringer, for the defence, said: "It will do no good to search in this case for heroes or villains, for there are only victims. There was not one fact, not one action, not one episode on Mr. von Bulow's part to suggest that he would do anything to hurt her."

The jury of five women and seven men considered their verdict for the next six days. On Tuesday, March 16th, 1982, they found Claus von Bulow guilty of two counts of assault with intent to murder. He was immediately freed on bail pending sentencing.

The verdict seemed to puzzle many people in the court. At one point it even seemed to puzzle the prosecution. Von Bulow's lawyer said: "I don't know if we will ever know how large a part his love affair with another woman took in this case, or even his aristocratic background and Danish citizenship. He took the verdict like a man. We intend to appeal."

And appeal they did, with satisfactory results. In June, 1985, Von Bulow was acquitted of trying to murder his wife. Two years later he brought a $20 million prosecution suit against his stepson Alexander Auersperg. But that was thrown out by US District Judge John Walker, who ruled that a statute of limitations had run out on Von Bulow.

The only question left then was who killed Sunny? The answer, probably, is that she killed herself, slowly, tortuously. The laxatives and aspirin and alcohol and drugs which she used to try to keep herself alive gradually eroded the life which she wasn't sure she even wanted anyway. For her, it was a classic case of affluenza.

13

TV'S COLONEL HOGAN
Murder, Sex and Videotape

Young actress Victoria Berry was slightly mystified as she approached the Winfield apartment-hotel in Scottsdale, Arizona. The actor she was going to see, Bob Crane, hadn't turned up for a lunch thrown for the cast of the play in which they were touring, and now, as she tried his apartment door, it opened at the touch of her hand.

Victoria knew that Bob Crane always double-locked his front door. Yet here it was clearly left unlocked.

Her 2.30 appointment with Crane that afternoon of June 29th, 1978, was to re-tape the soundtrack on a videotape of a scene from their play. Crane was helping her with the tape so that it could be sent to casting directors in the hope of securing work for her in Hollywood.

Bob Crane was a drummer-turned-disc-jockey-turned-actor. He had reached stardom and had become a household name in America as Colonel Hogan, the wisecracking prisoner of war in TV's *Hogan's Heroes*. Although his career had gone into decline after the long series ended, he was still able to make $200,000 a year touring in plays, which explained his presence at the Windmill Theatre in Scottsdale.

Victoria Berry pushed open the unlocked apartment door and was surprised that the inside was unusually dark. This was because the curtains were still drawn. She was also surprised to see a bottle of vodka and a half-empty bottle of Scotch on the table. She knew that Bob Crane drank little, limiting himself to vodka and orange, usually at nights.

She called out, and receiving no reply she went into the bedroom. At first she thought the prone figure on the bed was a woman with her hair standing on end. Calling Crane's name again, she immediately recognised his watch on the wrist of the body. Then she saw the blood.

Her screams brought neighbours running, and police arrived to find Bob Crane lying bludgeoned to death on his bed.

They noticed Crane's black bag, which had several zip-fastened compartments, was lying virtually empty beside him. It was Victoria who said that was unusual – Crane was a tidy, methodical man, and he always kept the bag in a cupboard. The bright blue key of his apartment was next to his wallet on the kitchen table.

There was no forced entry, which seemed to suggest to the police that Crane knew his attacker, and may have admitted him to the apartment before lying down on his bed.

But would he have lain down on his bed and gone to sleep while entertaining a caller? Another possibility was that the visitor had called and when he left had ensured that the door was unlocked, then waited for the actor to go to sleep and re-entered.

Alternatively, the caller could have surreptitiously slipped the lock on a window during his visit, subsequently climbing back in to kill the slumbering victim. The apartment was on the ground floor.

What was beyond dispute was that Bob Crane could never have known what hit him. This was apparently an extremely heavy instrument, like a tyre lever. The doctor who examined the body, Dr. Yens Karnitschnig, said the actor had been struck twice on the head while he was sleeping.

The pathologist added that the attack took place in the early hours of June 29th, and the depth of the skull-crushing wounds indicated that the killer was a man of considerable strength.

The first blow must have covered the weapon with

blood, yet there were only a couple of droplets on the ceiling and on the bedside lamp. That meant that the trajectory used by the killer as he brought the weapon crashing down on the sleeping man was a short one. Police reasoned that the killer was therefore male, for if a woman had swung the weapon with such force she would have had to use a wider arc, which would have flung much more blood on to the ceiling.

They also reasoned that the killer took his time. There was no sign of haste or frenzy. Crane had suffered extensive skull fractures and brain damage, and to ensure that the victim was dead the killer had tied a length of flex, taken from a video camera in the room, around the actor's neck.

As the investigation progressed, it appeared that this final touch with the video camera cord was symbolic. Nearly 50 videotapes were found in the apartment. They showed Crane having sex with a variety of women, prompting the suspicion that the killer was the husband or boy friend of one of the females on film.

The actor had set up a photographic lab in his bathroom, and a strip of negatives in the enlarger showed a woman clothed and then naked. It was speculated that the attacker took some black and white prints from this area, but overlooked the negatives. It was also theorised that he might have removed videotape of his wife or girl friend from the ransacked black bag found on Crane's bed.

Earlier in his career the actor had been contracted to star in the Disney movie *Super Dad*. The Disney organisation subsequently had misgivings about his image when an indication of his private predilections came to light.

Shrugging this off, Crane said that when they signed him the Disney studios did not know about his hobby of playing the drums in topless-bottomless bars.

"But what was wrong with that?" he asked. "I used to love sitting in with small groups to play the drums and naturally I liked looking at all those naked ladies. I'm a normal red-blooded guy and I was only looking at them – I wasn't doing anything with them. It just happened that they were at the places where I could play drums."

Crane's friends emphasised that he had never pressurised his videotape female accomplices to strip off and have sex with him in front of the camera, but his pastime seemed nonetheless out of place with the otherwise apparently well-balanced actor known to the public for his talent and his wit. A surprising number of Crane's women acquaintances had willingly accepted starring roles in his "home movies."

This interest was among the factors prompting his second wife Patricia Olson to begin divorce proceedings. Saying she was sick of his pornographic collection – in which she herself featured – she complained that he even tried to show blue movies to their six-year-old son. She also complained that when the little boy broke his arm Crane refused to take him to hospital.

Patricia had appeared with Crane in *Hogan's Heroes*, in which she played a fräulein. A week before her husband's death she visited him in Scottsdale so that the actor could see their son before she went to Seattle to appear in a stage play.

Crane had spoken to friends of a possible reconciliation, but they doubted that it would take place. Patricia's allegations in her divorce suit had devastated her husband, and he had not recovered from them. Wounded in particular by the complaints about his treatment of his young son, he was consulting a psychiatrist in an effort to become a better father.

At the same time, friends said, he was endeavouring to conceal his distress over the break-up of his marriage, taking refuge in playing the clown – a role in which he was adept. With the ready wit which once made him a popular disc jockey, he sprayed witticisms around like a fountain sprays water.

Yet he also continued to pursue his pornographic pastime, shooting videos and taking photographs of himself and countless women engaged in sexual activities. Victoria Berry said he had compiled a pornographic photo album which was "very graphic," and it might have pointed to the killer. But like the murder weapon which was carefully wiped clean on the bed sheets, the album was never found.

Did it contain photos of the woman whose husband or lover had turned killer? Commenting on the detectives' fruitless search for it, Scottsdale's police chief Walter Nemetz said that according to witnesses the album was "full of boring stills" which, like the videotapes, were nothing if not explicit.

Nemetz went on to say: "There were a lot of motives for this murder. Mr. Crane developed a lot of strange acquaintances because of his ... er ... er ... 'hobby.' His very peculiar activities off-stage could lead to many motives among his friends and acquaintances. These could include cuckolded husbands who heard about them. Possibly one of them went to the apartment in an attempt to retrieve a tape or tapes with his wife or girl friend in starring roles."

Until 2.30 a.m. on the night of the murder Bob Crane had been in the company of an old friend, John Carpenter, from Connecticut, who had since moved to Los Angeles and was in Scottsdale on business, taking the opportunity to see the actor at the same time. Because he was the last person known to have seen the victim alive, he became an instant suspect, and that suspicion was reinforced when he was reported to have left Scottsdale in a hurry.

Carpenter told detectives that his friend finished his evening performance as usual at about 10.30, and then followed his custom of remaining in the theatre lobby for a while to chat to fans and sign autographs. Two women were in the audience at Crane's invitation, and the star was to meet them later. But first he went to the Winfield apartment with Carpenter to drop off a few things, and while they were there he received a telephone call from Patricia, his wife, in Seattle.

According to Carpenter, the phone conversation became heated, developing into a shouting match which was loud enough for neighbours to hear Crane's end of the exchanges. The actor's hopes of a reconciliation seemed to have gone out of the window. But again according to Carpenter, Crane wasn't too worried by this because he had formed a new relationship with a pretty young blonde in Phoenix who he had already dated three or four times.

Carpenter and Crane then moved on to a bar in East Phoenix with the two women who had been in the theatre at Crane's invitation. At 2 a.m. the party went to the Safari Hotel in Scottsdale, and Carpenter said he last saw his friend outside the hotel's coffee shop half an hour later.

Carpenter told the police that he then left for his hotel, the Sunburst, to pack his bags in readiness for an early-morning flight back to Los Angeles. When he reached the hotel he phoned Bob Crane to say goodbye.

A hotel employee told detectives that Carpenter checked out "very hurriedly" and appeared nervous, demanding a limousine to take him to the airport in Phoenix, but only a cab was available.

At around 2.30 that afternoon Carpenter phoned the Windmill Theatre from Los Angeles asking for Crane. The member of staff who took the call told Carpenter that his friend wasn't there, and while Carpenter hung on the phone she called Crane's apartment, where Victoria Berry told her what had happened. When the girl relayed the news to Carpenter, he expressed his dismay and put down the phone.

Carpenter later told a reporter in Los Angeles, "I'm shocked. Completely shocked." He refused to say more until he had seen a lawyer.

Scottsdale's police force was a small one, with no homicide detectives. The department usually had nothing much bigger than a few burglaries and minor crimes to deal with, so there were no specialists on staff. They were soon accused of being out of their depth, and of bungling the investigation.

It was claimed that they carried out only a superficial survey of Bob Crane's dressing-room at the theatre, where one of the staff was given the job of collecting the actor's personal effects. Crane's eldest son Robert, by his first marriage, arrived on the evening of the 29th together with Lloyd Vaughan, the actor's business manager. Next day the police took them both to Crane's apartment at the Winfield, where officers handed them some beer and a bottle of wine from the refrigerator. Lloyd Vaughan later commented that these did not appear to have been checked for fingerprints, as they showed no sign of fingerprint-dusting.

Robert Crane and Lloyd Vaughan were then allowed to pack all Crane's possessions into suitcases, and it was reported that none of these items was checked for fingerprints. But it was possible that the police were keeping fingerprint information to themselves, in the event of the killer being arrested.

Only one hire-car at Phoenix airport was examined for missing or bloodstained tyre levers or wrenches, and many questions were left unanswered. Did the police try to check the source of the bottle of Scotch found in Crane's apartment? And as the actor didn't drink whisky, did detectives check his friends' drinking habits? Were all the women in the videotapes investigated, together with their husbands and boy friends?

Several cops in the Scottsdale police force were so upset by the apparently inept investigation that they switched their allegiance from the county attorney when he came up for re-election, pledging their support instead for a rival who promised a fresh inquiry. The county attorney was subsequently unseated, and his successor initiated the promised further investigation. But that also came to nothing, with the conclusion that there was insufficient evidence for anyone to be charged.

In the course of the second inquiry an unnamed woman suspect emerged, while some of the detectives involved remained convinced that they knew the identity of the killer, and that he was a man. They continued to be dissatisfied that no charges were brought against this man who they believed had bludgeoned Bob Crane to death.

Gary Maschner, of the Scottsdale police department, expressed the forlorn hope that the murderer would eventually confess, unable to continue living with his guilt. That, said Maschner, had been his experience with first-time murderers or random killers whose crime continued to play on their mind until they admitted what they had done. Maschner also believed that the person responsible for Bob Crane's death must have confessed to someone – "people need to talk."

It transpired that someone had in fact confessed – but it also quickly transpired that he couldn't have been the killer; he was unaware of evidence which the police had withheld from the public.

Two further theories were postulated. One favoured a contract-killing, carried out on the orders of a member of the Hollywood establishment whose wife or girl friend had featured in one of Crane's videotapes. Such a Hollywood tycoon, it was argued, would have the influence to arrange a cover-up even in faraway Scottsdale.

The second speculation focused on Scottsdale's hierarchy. It was suggested that Crane had inveigled the wife or girl friend of a pillar of the local establishment into appearing in one of his pornographic tapes. Such a husband or boy friend, it was speculated, would have the local string-pulling clout to suppress incriminating evidence.

Neither of these notions came to anything, however. Major Dave Townsend, of the Scottsdale police department, vowed that so long as Bob Crane's killer remained unknown, the file would stay open. And that's how it remains to this day.

14

RAMON NOVARRO
Horrific Finale to a Gay Afternoon

Anyone could have been forgiven for not believing that the mass of bloodstained, human flesh that lay on the bed had anything to do with the greatest heartthrob movie star of his generation.

Indeed, when the wide world heard the news it had some difficulty believing that Ramon Novarro, the man whose screen romances caused millions of women to swoon in his roles as the cinema's great Latin Lover, had been murdered.

Novarro was dead – and undoubtedly some of his legions of worshippers of the 1920s and 1930s, now grown to middle age, shed a silent tear or two as they recalled the dim and distant past they shared with him in cinemas with glitzy names like Roxy, Gaiety and Astoria. Only some of them, though, for Ramon Novarro, once the best known movie actor in Hollywood, was not only dead, but as a heartthrob he was almost completely forgotten.

There could be no greater contrast to the glamorous Hollywood life he had led than the shocking way of his death.

It was his secretary, Edward Weber, who made the discovery. Arriving at the 69-year-old actor's Spanish-style mansion in the Hollywood Hills on the morning of Thursday, October 31st, 1968, he looked forward to spending another day helping Novarro to complete his memoirs, chronicling a career which stretched back to his days as a breaker of hearts in silent movies of the early Twenties, through starring roles in such movies as *Ben Hur* and *The Prisoner of Zenda*, to his present-day roles on television.

But there was no remaining vestige of the actor's early days of swashbuckling glory or his comfortable middle-aged roles on the small screen as Edward Weber looked down in horror at his naked body which lay on the bed.

Novarro's hands were bound behind his back and his corpse was a mass of bruises. What looked like four fingernail scratches marked his throat. And the house in which he lived appeared to have been ransacked.

Scrawled on the bedroom mirror with a grease pencil were the words, "Us girls are better than faggots!"

Novarro's right hand was holding a rubber contraceptive, his left hand grasped a pen. A vibrator was thrust down his throat. Written on the bedsheet was the word "Larry," and on a pad on the bedside table "Larry" was scrawled four more times.

It was pretty obvious that Novarro was murdered by intruders looking for something to steal. It was also obvious that the murder had considerable sexual overtones. Those in the know in Hollywood wouldn't have been surprised at that. For the man who set millions of women's hearts racing in the flapper age was a homosexual.

Novarro – his real name was José Ramon Samaniegos – was born in Mexico in 1899, and it was his dark, flashing Mexican looks that caused him to be dubbed the Latin Lover. Civil war in Mexico drove his family to flee to California while he was still a boy, and as is often the case with immigrants, the next few years after that were tough.

But Novarro had a good singing voice and played the piano competently, and combined with his looks these talents got him jobs in vaudeville and night clubs. On one assignment he was spotted by one of the cinema industry's talent scouts who were proliferating in California in this early era of the industry. He was given roles in small films before making *The Prisoner of Zenda* in 1922, a film that turned out to be a smash-hit. Among the box office successes that followed were *The Arab*, *The Student Prince*, and the blockbuster *Ben Hur*, in which Novarro appeared stripped to the waist, revealing a body which drove his female fans wild with delight.

But the cinema sells dreams, and dreams they remained. The reality was far different. Off screen the Latin Lover's fancy was for young men with firm, muscled bodies, coupled with plenty of booze. The movie fans were not to know, of course, and Novarro's employers, MGM, put out smokescreens to ensure they didn't. Among one of the more incredible publicity stories pushed by the studio was that Novarro was a celibate student of philosophy who, but for his screen career, would have liked to have gone into a monastery.

Early in the 1930s Novarro successfully crossed a hurdle that brought down many a fine actor of the silent movie days – the switch to talkies. One of his best remembered talkies was *Mata Hari*, in which he starred alongside Greta Garbo. But by the end of the decade the fashion for dark-eyed, foreign-looking romantics had run its course and the fans were going for more realistic males like John Wayne, Leslie Howard and Clark Gable. Novarro began to bow out gracefully, playing middle-aged stage roles in the theatre and augmenting his huge screen fortune with a real estate business.

It didn't take long for police, called to Novarro's home by his distraught secretary, to pick up a lead to his murder. They discovered that at 8.30 p.m. on October 30th, the night of the murder, a 48-minute phone call was made from his house to a Chicago number. The call was traced to its recipient, 20-year-old Brenda Metcalf, who was not only able to tell the police that the call was made to her by a friend named Tom Ferguson, 17, but also vividly recalled what he said.

He told her that he and his 23-year-old brother Paul

were in Novarro's house. She said: "Tom told me that Paul had heard there were five thousand dollars in cash in the house. And he added: 'We are going to tie him up to make him tell us where it is.'"

During the conversation, she said, she could hear chilling screams in the background, like someone being tortured.

On Wednesday, November 6th, 1968, the two Ferguson brothers were arrested in Bell Gardens, a suburb of Los Angeles. They were booked on suspicion of murder and held without bail. Formal charges followed after it was discovered that fingerprints in Novarro's mansion left no doubt that the two brothers had been there.

The trial of Paul and Tom Ferguson began on Monday, July 28th, 1969, with Deputy District Attorney James Ideman making it clear to the court that he would seek a sentence of death in the gas chamber for Paul Ferguson – and that as far as the prosecution were concerned only Tom Ferguson's age would save him from the same fate.

He told the jury: "We will show that the Ferguson brothers were living in Gardena, a suburb of L.A. They were in need of money. Paul Ferguson was what is known as a hustler – a male prostitute. He would earn money by having sex with older men. The brothers were in need of much more money than could be obtained by any one sexual act. So Paul Ferguson came by the name of Ramon Novarro and phoned him.

"Now Mr. Novarro was a homosexual, but he did not go out in the streets and try to pick up people. The young male prostitutes would come to his home.

"Paul Ferguson called Novarro to try to get an appointment to see him, and gave the name of his brother-in-law as having referred him there."

Mr. Ideman said that the Ferguson brothers obtained a ride to Novarro's home from a friend on the afternoon of October 30th. They were received by Mr. Novarro and at first things went in a congenial manner. They drank together and had some supper. Later on, apparently, Paul Ferguson and Mr Novarro went into the bedroom. Some time between eight-thirty and nine p.m. Paul began demanding money from Mr. Novarro.

"He had very little cash and transacted most of his business by cheque. So there wasn't any money to give, and then Paul began to beat him. He was soon joined by his brother, who had been in another room."

Mr. Ideman said the actor was flailed with a silver-handled cane – a memento of one of his early movies. He was struck on the head and on his private parts. His nose was broken, one of his teeth was knocked out, and when he was in danger of losing consciousness and would be unable to tell the brothers what they wanted to know, he was led to a shower and revived.

"He was placed on his back on the bed, his hands tied behind him. In that position, unable to move and bleeding, he ultimately lost consciousness. Unable to swallow because he was unconscious, the blood drained down into his lungs, and he drowned in his own blood."

While Novarro lay dying the brothers ransacked the house looking for items of value. They found the actor's wallet, took $45 from it, and placed it under a corner of the mat in the bedroom. Then they stripped off their bloodstained clothing, replaced it with items taken from Novarro's wardrobe, and disposed of their own clothes in a nearby park – where they were later recovered by the police.

The prosecutor claimed that the two brothers then hitch-hiked back to Hollywood, and took a cab from there to their apartment in Gardena.

A wealthy estate agent with whom Paul Ferguson had lived at one time testified that on October 29th Paul Ferguson phoned him "and said he wanted some names – faggots to hustle."

"Larry," a relative of the estate agent, would receive phone calls at the estate agent's home from potential "customers," and these were the names that Paul Ferguson was seeking. "Among the names given to him was that of Ramon Novarro, together with his phone number."

The estate agent said that the two brothers came to his apartment late on the night of October 30th, or early in the morning of the 31st, that is, after they had been to Novarro's home. Tom Ferguson went to another room to lie down, and Paul began to describe what had happened. Paul said: "Tom went to bed with Ramon. Ramon tried to get funny with him, and Tom hit him several times and he is dead."

The witness asked Paul: "Where were you at the time this happened?" and Paul replied: "I was in another room, sleeping on a couch."

The evidence at this point was crucial to the prosecution's case, because after questioning the brothers when they were arrested the police had concluded that the killer was Paul Ferguson. Here, now, was a witness prepared to state that as a result of a conversation he had with Paul, the killer must have been Tom.

The witness went on to say that when Tom Ferguson woke up, Paul said: "Tom, I told what happened."

The witness said he then asked Tom Ferguson: "How could you do such a thing?' and the younger brother replied: "The guy made improper advances towards me. I just hit him several times and he is dead."

Brenda Metcalf, the girl Tom Ferguson phoned on the night of the murder, told the court that Tom told her he was in the home of Ramon Novarro. After some general conversation he said there was $5,000 hidden behind one of the pictures in the house. He also told her that his brother Paul was "with Ramon," trying to get the actor to tell him where the money was. She formed the impression during the conversation that both brothers were involved in the killing.

She repeatedly urged Tom Ferguson during their conversation not to do anything illegal, but when once he put down the phone for a moment she could hear loud screams in the background. When she asked him what they meant Tom was evasive, and said something about his brother trying to force Novarro into telling him where the money was hidden.

When Paul Ferguson gave evidence on his own behalf it was clear that there was about to be a struggle between the brothers as to who would take the blame for the fatal beating of Ramon Novarro. Paul faced the gas chamber, but if Tom admitted that he administered the fatal blows he could save his brother from execution.

However, if Tom could convince the jury that he had nothing to do with the actual killing, he might get off with manslaughter or second-degree murder, and a light sentence.

The court heard from other witnesses that Paul had been involved in homosexual activities with older men for money since he was nine years old. He was living apart from his wife and had an alcohol problem.

Questioned by his defence lawyer, Cletus Hanifin, Paul Ferguson denied ever hearing that there was $5,000 in Novarro's home, or that he went to the house with the intention of robbing the actor.

He said he phoned Novarro on the afternoon of October 30th. The actor gave him the address and said he would expect him at about 6 p.m.

"What was your real purpose in going to Ramon Novarro's home?" the defence lawyer asked.

"To earn some money."

"How did you expect to earn that money?"

"Hustling."

"By that you mean male prostitution?"

"Yes."

He said that when he and his brother arrived at the house Novarro steered them to an L-shaped couch, where they sat on either side of the actor. During the evening they chatted, played the piano, and "horsed around" with castanets. Paul Ferguson said that he himself drank more than a full bottle of vodka, and added that Novarro was also drinking quite a bit.

Paul said that while he and Novarro were playing a duet

at the piano, the actor asked him which of the two brothers was going to stay and which was going to leave. Paul told Novarro that he [Paul] was drunk, and asked if he could sleep off the drink.

Novarro said he could stay. Just before Paul passed out, he alleged that he saw Novarro and his brother go out on to the patio together.

"Did someone wake you?"

"Yes. Tommy."

"What did he say to you?"

"He said, 'This guy is dead.'"

"What did you do next?"

"I followed Tommy into the bedroom. Tommy said, 'See, this guy is dead. He's turned blue.' I touched him [Novarro] on the shoulder. It was starchy-like, you know, tight-like. Stiff, starchy. Like paper."

Paul quoted his brother as saying, "I didn't mean to do it," and claimed that Tom then suggested that they make the death look like a robbery.

Paul testified that Tom wrote on the mirror with a grease pencil while he wrote the word "Larry" on the bed and on the memo pad, but he denied that in doing so he had in mind the relative of the estate agent with whom he had once lived.

He said that his brother sat on Ramon Novarro's chest and scratched four marks on the actor's throat with a knife to make it appear that he had been scratched by a woman.

Mr. Hanifin asked Paul Ferguson if he expected to get any money from Novarro other than what he was to be paid for a sex act. The older brother said, "No." Then he was asked, "Did you have any sex with Mr. Novarro that night?"

"No, sir."

"Is there some reason you went along with your brother Tom to make this look like a robbery?"

"Stupidness."

During cross-examination he stuck to his story that he passed out on the couch, and when he woke up his brother told him that Novarro was dead. The reason he "lied and lied and lied" to the police after his arrest was because he was "trying to get out of this thing." But what he was now telling the jury was the truth.

Cross-examined by Richard Walton, defending Tom Ferguson, the older brother admitted that the thought had occurred to him that he might have killed Novarro during one of his drinking blackouts, but he said that doubt disappeared when Tom told him that he had committed the murder.

Paul said that most of the lies he told the police were to protect his brother, but the detectives "broke me down" after four or five hours of questioning.

"Then you decided to lay it on Tom?"

"I guess I did."

During his questioning of Paul Ferguson, Mr. Walton suggested that Paul was trying to "con" the jury into believing that his younger brother had committed the murder because he thought the courts would go easier on a juvenile. But Paul denied that after he and his younger brother left Novarro's home he discussed with Tom the possibility that Tom should take the blame for the murder, because he was too young to get the death penalty.

The jury heard the other side of this intriguing story, however, when Tom Ferguson was called to give evidence on his own behalf.

Tom insisted that it was his brother Paul, and not he, who had delivered the fatal beating. He said he was on the phone for nearly an hour, talking to Brenda Metcalf, while Paul was alone with Novarro.

"Did you murder him?"

"No."

"Did you participate in his death?"

"No."

Tom said that once during the evening when he wanted to use the bathroom he went through the master bedroom and saw his brother and Ramon Novarro naked together. When he completed the phone call to Chicago, Tom said, his brother called him from the bedroom. There he saw Novarro on the bed, "alive and conscious," but he appeared to have been beaten about the nose and mouth.

Tom said Paul directed him to help Novarro to the shower, and when he and the elderly actor were alone he warned him not to say anything to Paul, as his older brother would get violent.

Tom said he handed Novarro a towel. After the actor dried himself, he helped him back to bed, warning him again not to say anything to Paul.

Tom said he left the bedroom returning seven or eight minutes later, when he saw Novarro lying on the floor and looking as if he were dead. Tom testified that he never saw Paul strike Novarro, nor did he himself hit the elderly man.

Tom admitted that it was his idea to mess up the house, to make it look like a robbery-murder, that he scratched the throat of the dead man, and that he placed a condom in Novarro's hand.

He said he and his brother heard the news of Novarro's death the following morning on the radio. Paul persuaded him to accept the blame for the killing, since the older brother would face the gas chamber. But he changed his mind about taking the blame when he learned in court that the actor was viciously flailed with the silver-headed cane. He said he never saw the cane, and when the details of the beating were revealed, "it turned my stomach against Paul."

However, like Paul, Tom denied that there was ever any mention of $5,000 in Novarro's home. He claimed that he never told Brenda Metcalf in Chicago anything about it.

Cross-examined, Tom said Paul told him that when he went into the bedroom with Novarro the actor tried to kiss him, and that was when a vision of his estranged wife flashed in front of him. He told his younger brother that he shoved Novarro away from him, causing the actor to fall, injuring himself.

Mr. Ideman asked Tom: "How many times has Paul reminded you that he is facing the gas chamber?"

Tom replied: "About 300 or 400 times – maybe more."

Tom also claimed that he had been pressurised by people, including his mother, to take the blame for the killing.

The brothers' mother, giving evidence, said she had received several letters from Tom, in which he said of the murder, "He deserved to be killed. He was nothing but an old faggot," and that "we killed him."

In a letter to Tom she wrote: "Paul wrote to me the first trial day to say that everyone seems out to save his own skin and he is in a corner now. Tom, when you testify, think, think about what you are saying. I guess you are the only one who really knows the score. You are holding Paul's life in your hands... I'll keep my fingers crossed. Remember, after the sentencing it is too late to change the story, so make sure you realise what you are doing."

Another time she wrote: "I hope something happens for the better and lets Paul off the death sentence he feels he is going to get."

Despite the tone of her letters, she denied that she was attempting to persuade her younger son to take the blame for his brother. But in any event, Tom Ferguson steadfastly refused to change his story, insisting that he had nothing to do with the murder.

In his final address to the jury, Prosecutor Ideman described Ramon Novarro as a nice person, adding, "I hope sincerely you will not put Mr. Novarro on trial. He has paid for whatever he did and now it is the Fergusons' turn to pay for what they did.

"Brenda Metcalf from Chicago is the closest thing to an eye-witness that we have. You will have to decide whether or not she was telling the truth. Three people know exactly what happened in that house that night. Mr. Novarro is dead, so he can't tell us. Neither of the Ferguson brothers will admit to striking Mr. Novarro even once. As a matter of fact, after hearing the Fergusons' evidence, I was beginning to wonder if what we were dealing with was suicide.

"Mr. Novarro was trussed up like an animal and beaten to death. I don't think you would treat an animal like that. This was deliberate torture. You don't strike a man on his private parts and split his scalp with a cane unless you are torturing him."

Mr. Hanifin, in his final submission for the defence of Paul Ferguson, said his client had two defences. First, that he did not kill Ramon Novarro, that he went to the house strictly to hustle him; secondly, that he suffered from a mental illness brought on by alcohol. There was no evidence, in his view, to show that Paul participated in any act that would constitute torture.

Mr. Walton, for Tom Ferguson, insisted that his client played no part in the murder. He asked the jury to consider why Paul was nagged by the thought that he might have committed the murder, and why he was so obsessed with the thought of the gas chamber, if he did not kill Ramon Novarro.

Then he asked: "What would have happened that night if Paul Ferguson had not got drunk on Novarro's booze, at Novarro's urging and at Novarro's behest? Would all this have happened if Novarro had not been a seducer and a traducer of young men? The answers to these questions will determine the issue and degree of guilt of Tom Ferguson, and the issue and the degree of guilt of Paul Ferguson."

Mr. Walton argued that the elder Ferguson beat the victim after blacking out, and that he could not have formed the intent necessary for either first or second-degree murder.

After deliberating for three days, the jury convicted both brothers of first-degree murder. This meant that Tom Ferguson would automatically draw a sentence of life in prison. The fate of Paul would be determined at the penalty phase of the trial.

It was at this point that Ramon Novarro's friends might have reflected that the great Latin Lover had played some highly melodramatic roles in his life, but the trial that followed his death beat them all for sheer dramatics.

For when the penalty phase of the trial began Tom Ferguson completely changed his story, and in so doing revealed what was going on among the lawyers backstage.

Questioned by Mr. Hanifin he was asked: "Did you kill Novarro?"

He replied: "It was my fault that he died."

"Did Paul participate in Ramon Novarro's death?"

"No, sir."

Admitting that he had lied, Tom said he got mad at Novarro and hit him repeatedly with his fists while his brother was sleeping. He said he tied up the unconscious victim and awakened Paul. After he and his brother "messed up the house" he took money from Novarro's wallet and removed the victim's cane from a cupboard. He said, "At first I was just goofing around, twirling it like a baton, and then I walked into the bedroom and hit Novarro across the face with it just because I was mad. He was just like an old punk."

Tom told the jury that he finally decided to tell the truth because, "I don't want it on my shoulders if I send Paul to the gas chamber."

Asked by Mr. Ideman if it hadn't troubled his conscience when he blamed the killing on Paul, Tom replied, "Not a bit. He was supposed to get manslaughter, and I was supposed to get off. It's not our fault that we got a dumb jury."

Judge Mark Brandler asked, "What did you mean when you said you didn't kill him, but that you were responsible for his death?"

Tom replied, "He wasn't killed. He died of a broken nose, and I'm the one who busted his nose."

"Did you murder him, or participate in his death?"

"I caused the death ... he caused his death ... we caused his death," Tom replied. "He was as much a part of it as I was."

"Who's the we?" asked the judge.

"Mr. Novarro."

In his final speech Mr. Ideman labelled Tom's confession "a last-minute scurrying-about to create a doubt in your mind," and he urged the jury to vote for the death penalty for Paul.

But if Tom's scheme was to keep his brother from going to the gas chamber, and there can't be much doubt about that, it was successful. After two hours' deliberation the jury recommended life imprisonment for both brothers. But Paul Ferguson will have ample time to consider whether after all he was all that well served by his brother, and Tom Ferguson will have plenty of space to think about the "dumb jury" who did not come up with things quite the way the lawyers expected. For sentencing them, the judge recommended that both of them should never be freed on parole.

15

LEON TROTSKY
Killer Came Armed with an Ice-pick

As soon as he was outlawed from Russia, Leon Trotsky knew he was marked down to be murdered. Every day for 17 years he lived with that knowledge before it actually happened.

He did all he could to postpone, if not avoid, the inevitable. After fleeing from Russia he moved to Mexico, the only country in the world that would accept him. The Mexicans did a deal with him: he could live in Mexico and carry on with his brand of political agitation as long as he did not interfere in Mexican politics.

That suited Trotsky. At Coyoacán, near Mexico City, he moved into a villa which he quickly turned into a fortress to protect himself from potential Soviet assassins. It was built Spanish-style around a tree-lined courtyard and surrounded by high walls. He hired workmen to raise the walls and build look-out turrets in each of the four corners, in which he placed guards armed with machine-guns on a 24-hour roster.

There was no doubt that the villa was intimidating to would-be murderers. But it also had the effect of keeping its owner a virtual prisoner in his own home.

Trotsky's companions were his devoted wife and fellow-communist, Nathalie Sedova, and a score or so of loyal servants, mostly fanatical American communists, who looked after the fortress and formed his bodyguard. All were hand-picked and well screened, swearing allegiance to the former top Russian revolutionary boss and ready to die for him.

Here Trotsky lived out the cramped life of a fugitive politician in exile. In the tree-lined courtyard he kept a collection of tame rabbits, to which he devoted much attention. They were his only form of relaxation. The rest of his day was spent on writing political pamphlets and revolutionary literature which was eagerly devoured by his adherents across the world.

Here he attempted to prophesy a future world dominated by his own particular brand of communism in a new world order. Here, too, he had plenty of time to review a past which for him had gone all wrong.

Trotsky, or Lev Davidovitch Bronstein, to give him his real name, was born in the Ukraine in 1879, the son of a Jewish farmer. As a young man he was twice imprisoned for taking part in revolutionary activities. After he fled from his native country, Paris, Vienna, Switzerland and the Balkan states all knew him as an agitator who preached extreme doctrines and lived from hand to mouth on the slender earnings of his pen.

He was in New York in 1917 when he heard news of the Tsar's overthrow. He hurried back to Russia and arrived at the moment when the moderate politician Alexander Kerensky was just rising to the head of a provisional Russian government. Trotsky wanted nothing to do with that, and at once associated himself with Vladimir Lenin, leader of the Bolshevik faction. Trotsky's fiery oratory, tireless energy, and relentless preaching of the most extreme measures soon brought him to the fore.

When Kerensky was overthrown by the Bolsheviks in November, 1917, it was Trotsky who walked with Lenin into the party's headquarters to take over the government. He became minister of foreign affairs, then minister of war, and formed the famous "Red Armies" which defeated so many military attempts to overturn the Bolshevik government. He was the chief man of action in Soviet

Russia, as Lenin was its prophet and theorist.

But in 1924 Lenin died, and Trotsky's influence began to wane. A fierce rivalry developed between him and Josef Stalin. Trotsky wanted world revolution, a worldwide communist assault on capitalism. Stalin, on the other hand, was content to oversee the revolution in Russia. Soviet Communism required only one dictator – and the man who had to go was Trotsky.

That perhaps was inevitable, for Stalin was an iron-fisted politician, and Trotsky was an intellectual. His enemies stripped him of his power and in 1927 even dismissed him from he party. Stalin, now supreme leader, poured public scorn on his revolutionary record and had him arrested. Not murdered, as happened to most of Stalin's other enemies, but banished from Moscow and kept under close guard in Turkestan for the time being.

Stalin knew that Trotsky had armies of friends and vast influence – to have him killed might backfire. Aware that under the new regime millions of innocent Russians were being killed in sweeping political purges, Trotsky decided to escape from Russia.

His destination was Coyoacán in Mexico, where his followers were already preparing his siege fortress with its armed turrets. Although no fortress had ever been built that was proof against the NKVD, the Soviet secret police, he was left unmolested for several years. Then, with the threat of world war looming in Europe in the late 1930s, the Soviet leadership tightened its grip on the political machine. There could be no alternative leadership sprung on the country from outside as it drew near to its gravest hour. The order went out from the Kremlin: Trotsky was dangerous, and therefore must die.

Trotsky knew it was bound to happen, because he himself had founded the GPU, the first Soviet secret police, now called the NKVD. He knew that when the party machine ordered a murder, the secret police would not rest until it was achieved. He improved and increased the fortifications of his villa, and brought in armed guards to patrol outside. Doors and walls were reinforced, and steel shutters, closed at twilight, were added to the windows.

How Trotsky was eventually murdered is one of the most bizarre stories in the long history of political assassinations. It involved an armed siege, dozens of fanatics and some very curious characters acting under orders from the Soviet secret police.

First to arrive on the complex scene was an American named Robert Sheldon Harte. He was six feet six inches tall and had a shock of red hair, all of which made him easily recognisable if he were ever unmasked as a secret agent or would-be assassin. No one knows to this day precisely whether Harte was either of those things, or whether he was just a Communist drifter, because after meeting Trotsky he didn't live long enough to explain anything about himself.

Harte arrived at Trotsky's fortified villa in the spring of 1940 claiming to be a consummate Trotskyite, as followers of the exiled leader were known. He was an easy-natured, engaging sort of man and got past screening first by the Mexican police, who routinely checked all new arrivals to the Trotsky domain because they did not want any trouble there, and then by Fourth International devotees of the old revolutionary. So the genial, likeable Harte was accepted, and settled down as a member of the household, where he was apparently well liked.

That spring was to bring more visitors to the fortress. Next among them was a French couple, Alfred and Marguerite Rosmer. They came from France bringing with them Trotsky's small grandson Sieva, who had been at school in Paris. With France now over-run by the German army the Rosmers had smuggled out young Sieva in the nick of time and there was great delight inside the fortress when the boy arrived.

Yet another visitor was a man named Frank Jacson. He claimed to be a Belgian Trotskyite, although he had a Canadian passport. He was apparently a broker of

Mexican raw materials employed by a European company, and fancied himself as a political writer.

Jacson was introduced to Trotsky by the revolutionary's secretary, whose sister, Sylvia Ageloff, was a friend of Jacson's. We shall presently hear more of Sylvia, who had an important part to play in the plot. As a result of that introduction, Jacson too was accepted into the fortress community and, like the American Robert Harte, made himself useful doing household chores. Unlike Harte, though, he did not have a room in the villa. He called occasionally to talk to Trotsky and his wife, to make himself generally useful to the couple, and to occasionally produce some article he was in the middle of writing for the perusal of the aged revolutionary.

The Rosmers had decided that they would leave Mexico on May 28th, sailing from the port of Vera Cruz. But on May 24th the Soviet secret police decided to strike at Trotsky by the simple expedient of an armed attack on his fortress.

At about three o'clock in the morning thirty men, all dressed in the uniforms of the Mexican police, stormed the villa and literally threw themselves, SAS style, into it. They were led by a house painter named David Siqueriros, dressed in the uniform of a Mexican colonel. His second-in-command, Antonio Pujol, also a house painter, wore the insignia of a lieutenant.

No one ever found out where the raiding party got their uniforms. No one found out for sure how they knew that the gate in the villa courtyard had been left unlocked that night, but that was how they gained entry.

The attackers silenced all the guards, including those in the towers, without firing a shot, tying them up and locking them in a shed. But Harte, who happened to be on guard duty that night, was not tied up. He was led away at gunpoint and shoved into one of the parked cars outside the fortress. When he was thus safely removed, the attackers brought a machine-gun into the courtyard and opened fire on the room where they knew that Trotsky and his wife Nathalie were sleeping.

The bullets ripped across their bedroom like hailstones, dislodging plaster that showered on to their bed. The couple leapt up and crouched under the sill of the window as the bullets tore away at the walls all around them. Outside they could hear men shouting, boots ringing on concrete, the sounds of panic and pandemonium.

The Trotskys heard a cry from the next room and guessed that their grandson was hit. Even while the bullets were still flying above them they crawled into the boy's room. A bullet had hit him in the foot and the wound was bleeding profusely. Oblivious to their danger, the elderly couple did their best to soothe the boy's fright.

As suddenly as it had begun the raid, which had lasted five minutes, ceased. The Trotskys heard the sound of retreat, car doors slamming, headlights scanning the horizon. Then the raiders were gone.

The Mexican police – the real ones this time – were on the scene at daybreak and for the next few days they searched high and low for clues. One of their discoveries was that each man in the raiding party had been paid 250 pesos in cash, stuffed into individual envelopes. But the man they most wanted to interview, Robert Sheldon Harte, last seen being driven away by the raiding party, was nowhere to be found.

Trotsky steadfastly refused to believe that Harte was in any way linked to the attack. Despite his protests, the police searched Harte's room at the villa. They found a hidden key and traced it to room number 37 at the Hotel Europa in Mexico City. They also found a suitcase in the room, with a Russian label on it.

A check at the Hotel Europa produced some revealing information about Harte. Three nights before the raid he had used room 37, and with him was a prostitute.

The woman was speedily arrested. Interrogated at police headquarters, she sulkily admitted that she was with Harte, whom she did not know, that he had a great deal to drink, and that he had a lot of money on him. But he said very little about himself, and seemed anxious and nervous.

The Mexican police decided not without good reason that Harte had been paid by the NKVD to infiltrate the Trotsky fortress, to leave open the gate on the night of the raid, to arrange to be taken prisoner, and for all this he had been well paid. The escapade with the prostitute, they decided, was Harte's way of trying to forget for the moment what he knew was going to happen.

Leon Trotsky would have none of this. He refused to believe Harte was working for the NKVD, and insisted that the American was kidnapped because he was loyal. Given the circumstantial evidence, it seemed that Trotsky was either incredibly naive or reluctant to admit that his screening process had let in a traitor. Or it may just be that Harte's easy-going manner had impressed the revolutionary to the extent that he really couldn't believe ill of him.

On May 28th, four days after the bungled raid on the Trotsky fortress, the Rosmers, who had been sleeping in another part of the villa and were unharmed, were due to start out on their return journey to Paris. True to a promise he had made earlier, Frank Jacson arrived to drive them to the port of Vera Cruz. The Rosmers were not quite ready when he turned up at the villa, so Nathalie Sedova made him a cup of coffee while he sat chatting to her in the kitchen.

Nathalie especially liked Jacson, He was as amiable, friendly and relaxed as the giant American Robert Harte. In fact, although no one at the villa could possibly have known it, Jacson was a highly skilled NKVD agent – trained all his life to be friendly and amiable just so that he could perform the one task required of him by the Soviet Union. To meet that criterion, just about everything concerning Frank Jacson was falsified.

His Canadian passport was false – he had paid 3,500 dollars for it. His name was false – his real name was Jacques Mornard Vandendreschd. He wasn't a Belgian – he was born in Persia in 1904, although his father may have been Flemish. His mother, Caridad Mercader, was Spanish, and a fanatical Communist who had been a Russian secret police agent based in Paris.

Jacques Mornard, as he is best known, fought in the Spanish Civil War with the Catalan Red Militia. He was slightly wounded, then, on orders from Moscow, pulled out of the fighting line back to Paris, where his mother was operating as an undercover agent. There, in 1938, he began to be trained by his mother and her accomplices for the task that the Kremlin had assigned to him.

The first part of the assignment was in true cloak and dagger style. Mornard, or Frank Jacson as he now was, was instructed to get to know a girl named Sylvia Ageloff. She was to be vital in the plot because as we have seen one of her sisters was Trotsky's secretary and she herself was friendly with a band of Trotskyites in New York.

Sylvia had come to Paris from New York on holiday as part of a round-Europe trip. She had just given up her job as a clinical psychologist working for the New York Board of Education and was taking a well-earned break. Somehow Mornard befriended her and she became deeply impressed with him. The bond between them appeared to strengthen when to her great delight Jacson persuaded her to stay on in Paris. Money wouldn't be a problem, he said, for he could easily find her a suitable job.

He was as good as his word. Within days he had come up with a job for her, writing articles on child psychology for a publishing firm called Argus.

Sylvia revelled in her new role, for she was being paid three thousand francs a month for her articles. She did not seem to be unduly puzzled that she was never asked to meet the editors of Argus, or that the intermediary who paid her monthly cheque was always her friend Frank Jacson, the only man she knew in the publishing house. She did think it curious, though, that when she asked to see some of her work in print, she was always put off with vague promises.

One day Jacson told her that he had to go to Brussels,

where his mother was ill. Before he left he gave Sylvia the address where he would be.

To surprise him, Sylvia followed him a few days later. But when she called at the address he had given her, he was not there and was not known there. Confronted with this when he returned to Paris, he said he had changed his mind and gone to England.

In due course Sylvia decided to return to New York, and seven months later, in September, 1939, Frank Jacson arrived there and looked her up. In January, 1940, she and Jacson flew to Mexico, where she visited her sister in Trotsky's villa and introduced Jacson to the famed revolutionary. Now Jacson got down to the business of ingratiating himself with Trotsky.

He had succeeded so well by the time the Rosmers were to return to Paris that it seemed perfectly natural to everyone that he should give them a lift in his car to their ship, and at the same time leave the draft of another of his political articles for Trotsky to read.

Sylvia returned to New York and Jacson continued to visit the Trotskys throughout the summer of 1940. When Sylvia returned to Mexico in August she was surprised to see how much her friend had changed. She found him nervous and irritable.

"I'm living under great strain," he told her, without explaining what the strain was.

She was not to know of course that because the May attempt on Trotsky's life, involving Robert Harte, had failed, the Kremlin was now pressurising Jacson, its man next-in-line on the job, to get on with it and kill Trotsky.

On August 10th Sylvia and Jacson went to have tea with the Trotskys. Jacson told the revolutionary that he would bring another draft article back within a week. Trotsky sniffed – he didn't like Jacson's writing style and had no regard for his political skills, but he was too polite to say so.

When Jacson reappeared several days later with the draft article Trotsky didn't think much of it. He suggested some changes, some parts to be re-written, and apparently grateful for the advice, Jacson departed. He returned on August 20th, bringing the finished article with him.

He was let in by the yard gate and spotted Trotsky at once in the courtyard, feeding his rabbits. Watching them from a balcony overlooking the courtyard as they chatted for a moment, Nathalie Sedova thought Jacson looked pale. The phony Canadian asked for a glass of water, was offered tea, and declined, insisting on water. After drinking from the glass he followed Trotsky into the study and handed him the article.

Jacson wrote in longhand in French, which gave Trotsky, who was short-sighted, some problems. The old man bent over the script, peering at it through his spectacles. His visitor's hand slipped into his raincoat pocket, where he had hidden a mountaineer's ice-pick.

As Trotsky peered at the article, Jacson swiftly took the ice-pick from out of the pocket and brought it crashing down on Trotsky's head. With all the force he could muster, he drove the metal spike three inches deep into the old man's brain. Trotsky gave a stifled cry, pushed himself out of his chair and staggered out of the study, pouring blood and brain matter. He collapsed into the arms of Nathalie Sedova, who had rushed forward when she heard him cry out.

An American guard had also heard Trotsky's cry, and now came rushing into the study. He was confronted by Jacson, who drew a revolver. With commendable courage the guard smashed the weapon to the floor and felled the assassin with a single blow.

Jacson gasped out: "They made me do it. They've imprisoned my mother."

"They," whoever they were, had certainly not im-prisoned Jacson's mother, who was still held in the highest regard by her NKVD employers. They might, though, have threatened to imprison her if she did not persuade her son to kill for them. But like many killers, Jacson had a variety of stories to tell after his arrest, and each new one contradicted the last.

Jacson told the Mexican police that he was deeply in love with Sylvia, but when they confronted him with her, it was evident that his love was not reciprocated. She screamed abuse at him, accusing him, not without reason, of cultivating her so that he could get access to his victim.

Trotsky died the next day from the effects of the single head wound. Why Jacson chose such a barbarous weapon is difficult to imagine, since he had on him at the time of the killing the revolver he pulled on the guard as well as a foot-long dagger.

The police found $900 in cash in his pockets, proof enough that Stalin paid his murderers well.

The Belgian authorities eventually established to their own satisfaction that Jacson was not one of theirs – they thought he spoke French with a Swiss accent and didn't seem to know anything at all about Belgium. The Canadians found that his false passport was issued to a man named Babich who was born in Yugoslavia and had become a naturalised Canadian. Babich was killed in the Spanish Civil War while fighting for the International Brigade, who were known to surrender their passports to the Soviets in the event of death, so that they could be used again for espionage purposes.

While Jacson was being held in custody and Mexican police were continuing to investigate his background, someone tipped them off to search a small house on the outskirts of Santa Rosa, and maybe even do some digging there. The police arrived at the house well prepared, wearing gas masks and carrying axes.

They quickly noticed signs of freshly laid concrete in an outhouse and began to dig. They did not have to go very deep before they came to the body of a man – who in life, they reckoned, must have been a giant. He had been buried in lime, which had eaten away most of his face. Only a fraction of his hair remained – just enough to show that it was red.

Thus was revealed the fate of Robert Sheldon Harte, who evidently of no further use to his Soviet masters, had been shot and buried in the outhouse within an hour of being led away as a "prisoner" during the abortive fortress raid.

On April 16th, 1943, Frank Jacson was brought to trial in Mexico City under the name Jacques Mornard. Since the murder of Trotsky he had been on remand in custody, living like a millionaire in a luxury prison cell and, given Robert Harte's fate, probably marvelling at his luck at still being alive.

A great deal had happened in the three years since he killed Trotsky. The Russians had successfully defended Stalingrad and had fought valiantly to repel the German invasion – they and Josef Stalin were now world heroes and the murder of Trotsky no longer amounted to very much politically.

The court was left in no doubt about Mornard's mission, or who were his paymasters. But he never said a thing. He was sentenced to a maximum of twenty years imprisonment, and so that he would continue to remain silent, his Russian employers spent hundreds of thousands of dollars providing him with every material comfort he needed in prison. He was even allowed to take a common law wife.

Even so, Mornard clearly doubted his chances at the endgame. When he learned that the Soviets intended to spring him from jail, he leaked details of the escape plot to the Mexican police, obviously considering himself safer as a Mexican prisoner than as a free man on his way back to Soviet Russia.

On May 6th, 1960, with three months of his sentence still to run, he was released. As he walked out of the prison gates, two Czech officials were waiting for him with a Czech passport and tickets for a flight to Havana. It was said that he would stay in Cuba for a week before sailing to Europe and settling down in Prague.

That exit from the Mexican prison might have been the first step to a new life for Jacques Mornard. Or it might have been the first step to death...

16

GIG YOUNG
Four Weddings and a Double Funeral

Gig Young was a professional loser. He made his living as a movie actor losing girls to other men. Over the years Hollywood had cast him as the charmer who always lost out in the end – losing Doris Day to Clark Gable in *Teacher's Pet*, for example. She was just one of the many girls who threw him over and went off with someone else at the end of the film.

Hollywood saw him that way, and that was how he came to see himself. Yet he was highly regarded as an actor. "When you play a second lead and lose the girl," he once said, "you have to make your part interesting while not competing with the leading man. There are few, very few, great second leads in the movie business. Producers have told me I'm one of them. What that means of course is that I've been typecast throughout most of my career."

As a "second-fiddle" he had been well paid, he said, but it had "taken a toll on my personal happiness ... you play a loser long enough and you end up a loser – at least, you are convinced you are a loser." It was to such typecasting that he attributed three failed marriages, and perhaps he was right. Maybe those three brides, influenced by his screen image, decided they had chosen second-best.

So when at 64 Young took a fourth wife, 31-year-old Kim Schmidt, friends hoped things would work out better this time. They didn't. Within three weeks, on Thursday,

October 19th, 1978, Gig Young was found dead in his Manhattan apartment, a revolver in his hand, the corpse of his new bride at his side.

Each had a single bullet wound in the head, and the police lost no time in declaring that this was a murder-suicide pact – Young had shot his wife and then himself, in his case, through the mouth.

The apartment-house manager heard shots, but his suspicions weren't aroused until he noticed that the Youngs hadn't taken in the groceries left at their door hours earlier. The deliveryman had knocked but had received no reply. It was the manager, using his pass-key, who found the bodies, by which time the couple had been dead for five hours.

The manager was later to be asked why he hadn't gone to investigate when he first heard the shots, and his explanation seemed reasonable: the sound of gunfire in New York had become almost commonplace. It was a period of violence, and most people kept out of the way when they heard shots, because they didn't want to risk becoming involved.

On a bedroom shelf in the apartment stood the Oscar awarded to Gig Young in 1969 for his performance in *They Shoot Horses, Don't They?* He had won it as Best Supporting Actor – and being best supporting actor was really the story of his life.

So had the man destined never to make it to the top decided to put an end to his second-fiddle existence, taking his young wife with him?

His friends couldn't believe that. They pointed out that Gig was financially secure, he had a beautiful bride and was in the best of spirits. It was true that he had once been an alcoholic, as he was the first to admit, but that was in the past. He had not touched liquor for years, or so he said.

The truth was that no one who knew Gig could believe he had committed suicide.

Something else suggested that this was no suicide. Gig Young left no note. In a suicide pact that was highly unusual, said the pathologist who examined the bodies. Almost invariably partners in death feel the need to explain, to ask forgiveness.

Nor are their deaths an act of sudden impulse. They are usually talked about at first, planned over a period, the culmination of prolonged troubles, not the outcome of a marriage of less than three weeks.

Gig Young met Kim Schmidt in Hong Kong in 1977, during the filming of *Game of Death* in which she had a small part. She was also a script supervisor and had been working in that capacity in Hong Kong, mostly on Kung Fu movies in which she also had minor roles.

Born in East Germany, she emigrated as a child to Australia with her mother, who now phoned from Melbourne to say she could not believe the police account of her daughter's death. "I am certain that Kim was not killed by her husband," she said. "They must have been shot by someone else. My husband also believes that someone killed them, and so do all their close friends in America, judging from the letters I've received."

That view was echoed by the actress Colleen Camp, who got to know Gig and Kim while *Game of Death* was being filmed. She found it "almost impossible to picture Gig with a gun. It sounds as if there was a robbery and someone made it look like murder-suicide."

She recalled: "Gig was very happy while in Hong Kong and fell in love with Kim when they met on the set the first day. From then on they were always together."

Someone else who dismissed the idea of Gig handling a gun was his third wife, the actress Elizabeth Montgomery, who played the witch Samantha in the successful TV series *Bewitched*. "I couldn't even imagine him having a gun in his apartment," she said.

But the police could. They found three more revolvers concealed in the actor's flat, together with ammunition. But to whom the guns were registered was never disclosed.

That suggested that Gig's friends and even his relatives didn't know him as well as they thought. But nagging questions remained, as the police themselves were to admit.

"The question 'Why?' is still one we can't begin to answer," said Detective Richard Chartrand. "Friends and relatives tell us he looked fine. They thought he was happy, financially comfortable and never at a loss for work whenever he wanted it, either on the stage, TV or in films. Not only that, they had a dinner party at a local restaurant scheduled for eight o'clock that evening to celebrate their marriage. It seemed that Mrs. Young had dressed to go out..."

And so she had, in a green velour blouse and grey slacks, and wearing several rings and necklaces, although her husband wore just a plaid shirt and grey trousers.

The couple telephoned an order for groceries to be delivered by midday, which, as the detective said, suggested that their deaths were not premeditated. "When a murder-suicide like this is perpetrated, it is usually planned well ahead," he observed. "There is just no motive we can come up with."

But the couple's wedding on September 27th, according to Gig's newspaper-columnist friend Earl Wilson, was touch-and-go right up to the moment it took place. "He seemed very afraid of this marriage, nervous and fearful that it would not take place at all. He said, 'We're supposed to get married the day after tomorrow. but don't print it yet because it would be embarrassing if we didn't.'"

And after the wedding, a low-key affair in a judge's chambers, Young told the columnist: "Okay, Earl, we did it! But I don't want a big party this time."

That could be explained by the failure of his three previous marriages. But Young also told the columnist something else. He said there had been a serious row over something in Kim's past, and at that time they had decided to stay single.

In the three weeks following the marriage they were conspicuous by their absence from their usual haunts. Had they gone into hiding? And if so, from whom?

Could it be Harriet Vine Douglas, an ex-actress and

dancer whose 10-year relationship with Young ended after Kim came on to the scene?

It was rumoured among Young's friends that Kim was jealous of this long-standing affair. Perhaps there was good reason for her to be. Harriet divorced her Broadway actor husband in order to live with Gig, and although her relationship with him was now apparently over, the former lovers still remained in touch.

It is known that Harriet spoke to Gig only a week before he died. He told her he had declined to sign a document drawn up by his business manager in which Harriet would relinquish any claim on his estate.

According to Harriet, he had left a signed will with her in it, and an unsigned one from which she was excluded. Had this been a cause of dissension between Gig and Kim?

Just how close 58-year-old Harriet had been to Young became apparent when she arrived from California to make the funeral arrangements with the consent of his sister. "I want him remembered with dignity and not as a murderer," she said. But as she talked a possible motive for the couple's death began to emerge.

She disclosed that some months before the wedding she drove Gig to Los Angeles airport to meet Kim off a plane from Hong Kong. On the way she advised him: "Go to New York and live with her, but don't marry her." He had replied: "Don't let any crazy things I do spoil our relationship."

Two months after that the veteran actor and the bit-part actress half his age became engaged. But Gig was not in the best of health. He had aged following a heart attack in 1970, and now a mild skin cancer caused by the Californian sun prompted him to cut his ties with Los Angeles. He decided to move permanently to the apartment he already owned in Manhattan. This entailed a move for Harriet as well – he asked her to sell the Los Angeles home they shared, which she did at a good profit.

Arguments followed, however, over the division of their furniture, and Kim, the bride-to-be, was present at these scenes.

"Kim was so jealous she didn't even want an ashtray from the apartment I'd shared with Gig," said Harriet. "During one discussion Gig and Kim began quarrelling over some lamps, and Gig snapped at her."

Harriet added that she cautioned Young not to phone her behind Kim's back, but to keep everything out in the open. She also had some advice for Kim, telling her not to let Gig start drinking again.

If this seems an odd set-up for a couple about to be married – with a former lover acting as a sort of consultant and evidently intending to stay in the frame – that, said Harriet, was the way it was.

Although Young had been short with her for a time, Harriet said, he had mellowed when she last spoke to him. "You coming home, baby?" she had asked him, convinced that he would return to her in the long run.

So if there was trouble between Gig and Kim just after they were married, was the source an old flame biding her time in Los Angeles?

Even if the answer to that question is yes, there were still other questions unanswered. Why, for instance, did the Youngs order groceries and arrange to entertain friends at dinner in a restaurant that night if they planned a suicide pact?

Why was Gig in casual clothes, while his wife was dressed for dining out?

What was it in Kim's past that earlier almost caused the couple to split up? Had it resurfaced, refusing to go away, and causing the couple to think about parting? Had its refusal to go away led to a suicide pact?

Did Kim tell Gig she was leaving him, because she resented Harriet and was tired of the continuing quarrels? And did he consequently shoot her and then himself, unable to live with the thought of becoming a loser once again?

Or was there an unknown assailant who arranged the bodies to suggest a murder-suicide? If so, who? There was no evidence in Gig Young's life that he had that sort of enemy. So, in the absence of any signs of a struggle, the police stuck to their theory of a murder-suicide pact.

Friends continued to insist that there was no way Gig would have become involved with guns, despite the four found in his flat. In the few cowboy films in which he appeared, he was scared even when he had to fire a weapon loaded with blanks. So were the guns Kim's? Did she bring them with her from Hong Kong for some reason best known to herself? That is a possibility, because all this happened in the days before airport baggage X-ray checks.

That aspect of the case could have been resolved for us if the investigators had divulged in whose name the guns were registered, assuming, that is, that they were licensed. But the police weren't talking. Something else they never revealed was what evidence they found of powder burns, or whether there were any tell-tale traces of gunpowder on Gig's hand, which would have been the case if he fired the revolver he was holding.

These things alone would have cut short the public debate on whether this was murder or suicide. So why did the police say nothing?

Just as the revolvers in his apartment contrasted with the gun-shy man his intimates thought they knew, so did the tributes paid to Gig Young conflict with another person's experience. He was generally regarded as a good man, a man easy to like, with no enemies.

But the daughter he had not seen since she was four years old told a different story. Three years after his death, when she was 18, she recalled that when he appeared on television she would slap the screen in anger. Describing how she would cry herself to sleep, she said, "I never heard from him, not even on my birthday or at Christmas.

"And when I saw him on television I used to scream at the box, 'How could you leave me?'"

So were there two Gig Youngs – the easy-going public persona and a dark, secretive character who few people knew lurking within him? If that is true, that other character would surely also be an Oscar nomination for Best Supporting Actor.

17

MARVIN GAYE
Big Daddy and the Prince of Soul

No one familiar with the golden boy of Soul music, the debonair Marvin Gaye, known as the Prince of Motown, would have recognised the middle-aged man sprawled on a bed in the Los Angeles house he had bought for his parents. On the eve of his forty-fifth birthday the once handsome, athletic black singer was a physical wreck, crazed by cocaine and a haunting obsession.

Gaye was convinced that someone was out to kill him. In readiness, he kept a gun under his bed. Another was to hand in his bathrobe pocket.

Friends dismissed this as a drug-induced, paranoid delusion. True, he had enemies. But in the cut-throat world of pop music, who hadn't? And despite his turbulent private life and his rancorous professional relationships, he was still loved even by those he had crossed. They regarded him with a sympathetic, despairing affection.

Yet someone would kill him, he insisted, and he was to be proved tragically right. He never made it to that forty-fifth birthday. On that fateful Sunday, April 1st, 1984, he had enough problems to engage a whole league of Samaritans.

Marvin Gaye was a boy from nowhere who became the idol of millions, the Prince of Motown, and couldn't handle it. (For the uninitiated Motown is a record company label, whose name is a corruption of "motor town," meaning Detroit). Now he was bankrupt, his career and two marriages in ruins, his creditors hounding him for more than $5 million.

It must have seemed to him that nothing had really gone right from day one. That was April 2nd, 1939, when he was born in Washington DC, the son of a Pentecostal minister who couldn't stand the sight of him.

While the young Marvin was to achieve extraordinary success, his father, who was no less extraordinary, was almost totally unsuccessful. A religious zealot, the minister had embraced a faith which required women to keep their hair hidden under a white head-dress on the Sabbath. His Church also forbade youngsters to enter cinemas and dance-halls. It even banned sleeveless dresses.

The minister himself observed a peculiar dress-code. He often wore his wife's clothes, including her stockings and undies, and for a while he grew his hair long, sometimes also wearing a wig. The religious justification for this was obscure. His wife said he simply enjoyed wearing her things. Young Marvin didn't enjoy being teased at school about his father's habits, and he enjoyed even less the frequent thrashings he received from the minister.

His father, though, seemed to revel in handing out punishment. "Boy, you're going to get a whipping," he would say. Then he would prolong the agony by keeping Marvin waiting naked for an hour, listening to the minister's belt-buckle jangling.

The boy's mother, Alberta, was later to say that her husband didn't love Marvin and didn't want her to love him either. "Marvin wasn't very old before he understood that."

Nevertheless, Alberta Gaye did her best to compensate for the father's lack of affection. She spoiled her young son, unwittingly leading him to expect the same indulgence from the women he was to know later in life.

She was also the family's breadwinner. The minister was congenitally idle, so to support her four children Alberta got up early every day to work as a cleaner in Washington's white suburbs. Marvin fantasised about raiding banks to spare his mother "cleaning rich people's toilets for slave wages."

While his imagination had him robbing banks, however, reality required his presence at church services. It was on these occasions that he discovered he could sing – with such feeling and talent as a boy soprano as to incur increased displeasure from his father. The minister took a dim view of being upstaged by his son. "He hated it when my singing won more praise than his sermons," said Marvin.

As time passed the minister made two career moves, neither of them propitious. When his Church split into opposing factions he backed the loser. Finding he had no congregation, he rejoined the mainstream, and then felt that he was being passed over for promotion. Disgruntled, he replaced his allegiance to God with an addiction to vodka.

Meanwhile, young Marvin was becoming a talented musician, learning to play a variety of instruments by ear, without tuition. His singing was also attracting attention and his taste in music was broadening. Hymns gave way to romantic lyrics, and he discovered the power his love songs gave him over girls.

When he gave concerts with school friends his father warned him: "You're running around with bums, and you're going to end up a bum." Having never given Marvin the slightest encouragement to do anything, the minister coupled these warnings with more beatings. By now the boy was bigger and stronger than his undersized, effeminate parent, but he took the thrashings without protest. He was later to say, "Where I come from, even to raise your hand to your father is an invitation for him to kill you."

The minister's harsh discipline, however, made him a rebel. He dropped out of school at 17 and joined the US Air Force. But instead of becoming a dashing pilot he found himself peeling potatoes. Eight months later he was discharged, the air force finding him unable to "adjust to regimentation and authority." That judgement was to apply for the rest of his life.

Meanwhile he had his first coupling with a prostitute, who deprived him of his virginity with a brusque efficiency that both shocked and excited him. Hookers were to have an enduring role in his life after that. They protected him from passion, he was to remark.

Back in Washington, he quickly found that it was no place for a budding black musician. There was a conspicuous lack of facilities and opportunities, as he discovered when he teamed up with friends to form a group called The Marquees. But it was in Washington that he was talent-spotted in 1958 by the up-and-coming black singer, songwriter and entrepreneur Harvey Fuqua.

When Fuqua put The Marquees under contract, impressed by their style, Marvin pictured himself "singing before thousands of women, making them swoon, choosing any one of them just for the asking." It was an extravagant daydream, but before long it came true.

For all his apparent confidence, though, Marvin suffered from stage-fright. His fear of crowds was to dog his whole career. He was only truly at ease in recording studios, singing to a microphone instead of his imagined thousands of swooning women.

Moving from Washington to join Fuqua's operation in Chicago, Marvin was sent on tour with The Moonglows, whose act also featured a dancer with the intriguing name of Titty Tassel Toni. The two were soon involved in a heady romance that was as brief as it was passionate. In one of their squabbles Toni bit Marvin's chest so badly that he needed hospital treatment, complete with stitches and a tetanus injection.

At about this time Marvin was introduced to drugs. He became an addict, he was later to say, because he hated drinking – an aversion inspired perhaps by the example of his father.

The following year Fuqua disbanded The Moonglows and moved Marvin to Detroit, the "Motown" created by Berry Gordy, Jr, a promoter dedicated to getting black music accepted wherever music was played. This was the rock, rhythm-and-blues and soul scene that was to spawn such stars as Stevie Wonder, Diana Ross and The Supremes – and Marvin Gaye.

Fuqua not only linked up with Gordy professionally, he also married his fellow-promoter's sister Gwen. Gordy took over Marvin's contract with Fuqua, engaging him primarily as a pianist and drummer, with a bit of songwriting on the side.

Anna Gordy was another of Berry Gordy's four sisters. She took a fancy to young Marvin, 17 years her junior. And despite the age-gap he took a fancy to her – not least, he admitted, because he realised that she could advance his career. Through her influence he made his first records. They were immature and consequently not successful – he had still to "find himself," he said later.

He married Anna in 1962. She told him he was stubborn, and that remark gave him the idea that was to produce his first hit, *Stubborn Kind of Fellow*, written in collaboration with another songwriter and with a little musical help from Berry Gordy. More hits followed, enabling Marvin to move his parents into a better house in a more salubrious district. Alberta was no longer needed to do other folks' cleaning. Marvin was making good at last.

Mopping his brow on stage, he would throw the damp handkerchief to the audience and smile as his fans fought over it. That vision of bewitching all who heard him was being realised for the singer whose voice seemed to address every girl in the audience. He was making love to them, and they were entranced.

Yet behind his facade of apparent self-confidence Marvin Gaye remained a frightened performer, as Gordy was reminded at a Detroit night club when the singer's nerve failed him and he refused to go on. Gordy left his seat in the audience to go back-stage, where he slapped Marvin's face – hard. It did the trick. Within minutes Marvin was giving a flawless performance.

By now, with several hits behind him, he was in a strong position to refuse to take coaching at the charm school Gordy set up for all his performers. Marvin would probably have dug his heels in anyway, whether or not he was making hits. His rebellion was accepted not only because he was married to the boss's sister but also because his natural charm was recognisable. He didn't need any lessons.

But he could have done with counselling to enable him to overcome the kind of fear that paralysed him on his way to a New York engagement. On landing he immediately took the next plane back to Detroit.

Marvin wore a rubber band around his wrist, a reminder to himself that "material possessions were not all that important." That didn't stop him keeping three ritzy cars, including a Rolls-Royce and a Cadillac, in his garage. Despite all the big-time, though, marriage with Anna – they now had a son – was under strain.

The primary cause was mutual infidelity, which was leading to violence, but Anna was also jealous of Marvin's female co-stars – beautiful vocalists like Tammi Terrell, with whom he invariably said he was in love when they sang together. In fact, though, their association was never closer than that.

During a concert in 1967 Tammi suddenly collapsed. Marvin caught her as she fell, and carried her off-stage. A brain tumour was rumoured, operations followed, and she died three years later.

Marvin meanwhile moved up from marijuana to cocaine, sometimes snorting so much that he thought he would be dead in a matter of minutes. "I rather liked the idea of there being nothing left of me but my music," he recalled.

Suicide became increasingly attractive. Retiring to a Detroit apartment with a gun for company, he told anyone who approached that he was going to shoot himself. All attempts to talk him round were fruitless until his father-in-law, Berry Gordy, told him to stop acting the fool and to hand over his gun. Marvin meekly obeyed.

Now nearing 30, he was writing and singing songs reflecting the increasing pain of his marriage with all its betrayals and rage. *I Heard It Through the Grapevine* became the biggest hit in Motown's history, selling nearly four million discs. He bought his father a Cadillac, but decided against inviting him to visit Detroit. Neither really wished to see the other, and the ex-minister, as he now was, showed no gratitude for the gift. It seemed that although he was happy enough to use it, he resented being given it by the son he had detested from birth.

Cocaine continued to rule Marvin, although his health improved when two footballer friends, players with the Detroit Lions, persuaded him to join them in work-outs. Their influence and help did him nothing but good, but it wasn't to last.

When Marvin produced a new album, this time reflecting despair over racism, poverty, war and pollution, Motown Records were critical. For months they refused to release it, arguing that it was unlikely to be a commercial success. But when it eventually came out in 1971 Marvin Gaye was vindicated by the enthusiastic response, and he started collecting awards.

Inevitably he felt the bidding finger of Hollywood. He rented an apartment in Los Angeles, writing the score for the film *Trouble Man.* The spin-off album became another hit.

Setting aside their marital problems, he and Anna bought a ranch-style house in the Hollywood Hills, and for his parents Marvin bought a large home near the Santa Monica Freeway. The Santa Monica house was to become his bolt-hole, in spite of his father, who was now usually befuddled by vodka, no longer sleeping with Alberta and shocking her with his profanities. The entire family had become dependent on Marvin's money, and he could never bring himself to refuse them.

During a quiet spell in his career he made an album in which he was twinned with a pregnant Diana Ross, who was having trouble in her marriage. She was off-form, outshone by Marvin, and the venture was no more than a modest success.

Shortly afterwards Marvin was recording another album when the girl of his dreams walked into the studio. Janis Hunter, daughter of a black musician and a white woman, was the finest girl he had ever seen, Marvin told the other musicians. The arrival of Janis seemed to infuse him with new vigour. When he sang, "There's nothing wrong with me loving you," he sang it for her. She was an impressionable 17-year-old and his for the asking.

The album, released in 1973, was the biggest success of his career, such a money-spinner that Berry Gordy didn't quibble over Marvin's request for a new contract and a $1 million cheque. Then, instead of departing on the concert tour that customarily followed the release of a hit, the singer took off for the mountains with Janis.

He rented a rustic lodge in a canyon north-west of Los Angeles, a place reached only by twisting dirt roads, and in that mountain paradise he remained sequestered with his mistress for more than a year. While his wife Anna was 17 years his senior, he was 17 years older than Janis.

Anna was enraged, but Marvin didn't care. He felt above the world, he was to recall – "our happiness was all that counted," he said. But that fat cheque from Motown didn't change the fact that he still needed to earn a living, and he knew that splitting from Anna would cost him a fortune.

So, driven by financial necessity, Marvin came back to civilisation to play to huge audiences. But his concerts' overheads were breathtaking ... as was the five-acre estate he bought, complete with mansion, the new home he would share with Janis. By late 1975 they had two children, and far from becoming more prudent, he splashed out on his own luxurious, state-of-the-art recording studio in Hollywood, complete with apartment above.

His new home and studio absorbed that $1 million cheque and then some, and the split with Anna proved every bit as expensive as he feared – $66,000 a year, plus $25,000 legal costs.

Cash continued to flood in with royalties and recordings, but it also continued to ebb away just as swiftly, spent on Marvin's hangers-on, his 14 cars and the purchase of yet another house. Colossal sums also went on his cocaine habit and the countless hookers he took to that apartment over his studio.

As usual he sought to avert financial disaster with another tour – this time of Europe. Stage-fright almost got the better of him again and he tried to back out, pleading that as England was suffering a drought it would not be right for him to make things worse by drinking the country's water! But the tour went ahead and it was successful, although the hangers-on made sure it wasn't quite the money-spinner he expected.

He was also having trouble with Janis. She too wanted to sing, but he told her there was room for only one vocalist in the family. Anna demanded and got the equivalent of $1 million in final settlement of her divorce, which left him free to marry Janis, who was now 21, in 1977.

Debts continued to escalate, forcing him to file for bankruptcy four months after his marriage. He was estimated to owe nearly $7 million. His five-acre estate and his recording studio had to go. His career was also in decline, with no hits in 1978 or 1979.

Next, fights with Janis prompted her to move out with the children to her mother's home. When he went to see her she called the police, thinking he had come to snatch the kids. Officers ordered him to leave, there was a scuffle, and he ended up in hospital.

Time and again Janis returned to him, only to leave when he kept pressurising her to sleep with other men and describe her experiences. She ultimately had an affair with a young singer, and in September, 1979, she petitioned for divorce. After touring Hawaii, Marvin decided to settle down there, begging Janis to visit him with the children. She did so, but soon regretted it.

"All we did was fight and scream and scratch at each other," Marvin was later to say, confessing that at one stage he came near to knifing her through the heart.

Janis took off again, but this time she left their four-year-old son with him. As soon as she was gone Marvin snorted a massive dose of cocaine, then phoned his mother to say he was dead. The dependable Alberta, the only woman he knew would never betray him, was soon at his side with jewellery to pawn for her son.

January, 1980, saw the arrival in Hawaii of the British promoter who organised Marvin's European tour and who now hoped to arrange another. He was shocked to find the Prince of Motown living with his child in a broken-down bread-van, half starving, but still finding enough money to snort coke. For the time being a European tour was out of the question. Marvin Gaye could scarcely stand up.

Helped by the singer's mother, the promoter persuaded Marvin to return from his self-imposed exile. The Prince of Motown was slowly restored to better health, and the following summer the European tour went ahead. But Marvin was still depressed, still taking worrying amounts of drugs, which now seemed to be all that kept him going.

The grand climax of the tour was to be a country club concert near London preceded by supper with Princess Margaret, the event's guest of honour. It never took place. When Marvin should have been dining with the princess he was lying naked on his hotel bed stoned almost out of his mind, telling the promoter to cancel the event. The royal party departed.

Marvin eventually arrived at the club when almost everyone had gone home. As he sat down at the piano to play, the curtain was brought down by the club's disgusted cleaners.

The tour's promoter was furious and said he was through with Marvin. When newspaper headlines blazoned the soul singer's snub to royalty, Marvin wanted to know why a prince should apologise to a princess.

He stayed on in London, now finally divorced by Janis and spending the money he received from the tour on women and drugs. A Belgian promoter came along with ideas for a tour of the Continent. Marvin needed the money, and the tour went ahead. Those who saw him at around this time were worried by his drawn, puffy-eyed appearance. Visitors to the apartment that became his base in Ostend also noted that it was stacked with pornographic magazines.

This prompted one caller to comment that what the singer needed was "sexual healing." Those words became the inspiration for Marvin's song of that title which occupied the top Soul slot in the charts for four months. Then Marvin parted company with the Belgian promoter who had done much to help him back to health and success. After nearly three years in Europe – where friends thought he should have stayed – he returned home to be with his mother, who was convalescing after a major operation.

His father returned to Washington a month before Alberta went into hospital, and stayed there. Marvin said his mother should have divorced him years ago, but he was nevertheless pleased by his father's absence. In January, 1983, however, the ex-minister returned to Los Angeles.

The old man had sold the house in Washington that Marvin bought for his parents and now refused to give his wife her share of the proceeds. This so annoyed Marvin that father and son were soon at loggerheads. The atmosphere in the house became so unpleasant that the singer's sister Jean moved out.

Now Marvin's career was on the slide again. His audiences were getting thinner by the week, and on stage he stripped to his underpants to give his performance of *Sexual Healing* every possible meaning in his desperation to woo fans.

Behind the stage he had a supply of drugs in one room and a clergyman in another, plying between the two in his increasingly frantic quest for help. And Marvin sure needed help, his musicians decided, when he blandly told them that "killers' were out to shoot him. Friends watched in disbelief when he stationed armed bodyguards on stage and outside his hotel bedroom, and when he took to wearing a bullet-proof vest.

The long suffering Janis came to see him during this American tour, just as she came to see him when he was in Europe, but their reunions were always acrimonious. This time he hit her. The tour ended prematurely in Florida when he was taken to hospital suffering from exhaustion. When he went back to his mother's home she thought he was more sick than she had ever seen him. He shut himself up in the room next to hers, taking drugs and visited by dealers and hookers.

Alberta begged him to get rid of his pistols. When a sub-machine-gun was delivered she hit the roof, and in his fury Marvin hurled the weapon through the closed window. A telephone went the same way. His sister-in-law next door thought he had gone totally mad. On a rare excursion from the house he threw himself in front of a car, which swerved and only just missed him.

Down the landing from the singer's room his father sat swigging vodka most of the time. But on Sunday morning, April 1st, 1984, the ex-minister was downstairs, prowling the ground floor in search of an insurance letter he had mislaid.

As the old man's irritation mounted, he called out to his wife, "Where's that damned letter? You must have seen it."

Alberta was in Marvin's room, at the foot of his bed, keeping her son company although she was still weak from her operation. Unable to hear distinctly what he was saying, she asked him to come into Marvin's room.

"No, I won't do that," her husband shouted.

"If you don't come in here now, you'll never enter this room again," Marvin called back.

At that, the ex-minister opened the door. Marvin got up,

told him to get out, and started pushing him. The father went back to his own room followed by his son, who was now swearing at him and threatening to beat him up.

Alberta heard them go into the old man's room and she heard her husband call out, "He's kicking me! I don't have to take that!" Then she heard Marvin hitting her husband, who was on the floor when she went to them. She took her son by the arm, led him back to his room and sat him on the foot of his bed. He told her he was leaving: "Father hates me and I'm never coming back."

At that moment the door opened again. The ex-minister stood on the threshold, holding the .38 revolver he usually kept under his pillow. He said nothing as he calmly pointed the gun at Marvin and fired. His son screamed and collapsed. The old man advanced further and shot his son again. But the second bullet was superfluous – the first had passed through Marvin's heart.

The singer's father went downstairs, chucked his gun on to the lawn and sat down to wait for the police.

A mile-long queue of more than 10,000 mourners filed past Marvin Gaye's open coffin at Forest Lawn Memorial Park the night before his funeral. Marvin lay on his back, wearing the white and gold fancy military uniform that was his costume on his last tour. As befitted the Prince of Motown, there was a wrap of ermine around his shoulders.

His old friend and rival Stevie Wonder sang at the service, which Marvin's mother, ex-wives and three children attended. Following the cremation, Anna and the children took the ashes out to sea and scattered them on the waves.

In prison awaiting trial, Marvin Gaye Snr, was asked if he had loved his son. His reply was carefully worded: "Let's say that I didn't dislike him."

Doctors who examined him discovered a tumour at the base of his brain. Although it was benign, it was in an area known to affect the emotions. Following an operation to remove the tumour he was found fit to stand trial, and Alberta arranged bail. At the same time she filed for divorce.

As the pause between the two shots suggested premeditation, Marvin's father was charged with murder. Photographs of bruises on the old man's body, however, persuaded the judge to accept a guilty plea to voluntary manslaughter. Marvin Gaye, Snr, was given five years' probation.

Released from jail, he returned to the house his son had bought and renewed his acquaintance with vodka. Before long, however, he was consigned to a nursing home. There he was last heard of walking around naked – except for a bra!

Alberta Gaye died three years later from bone cancer. But not before she uttered a fitting epitaph for the Prince of Motown. "If Marvin found happiness," she said, "he always found a way to lose it."